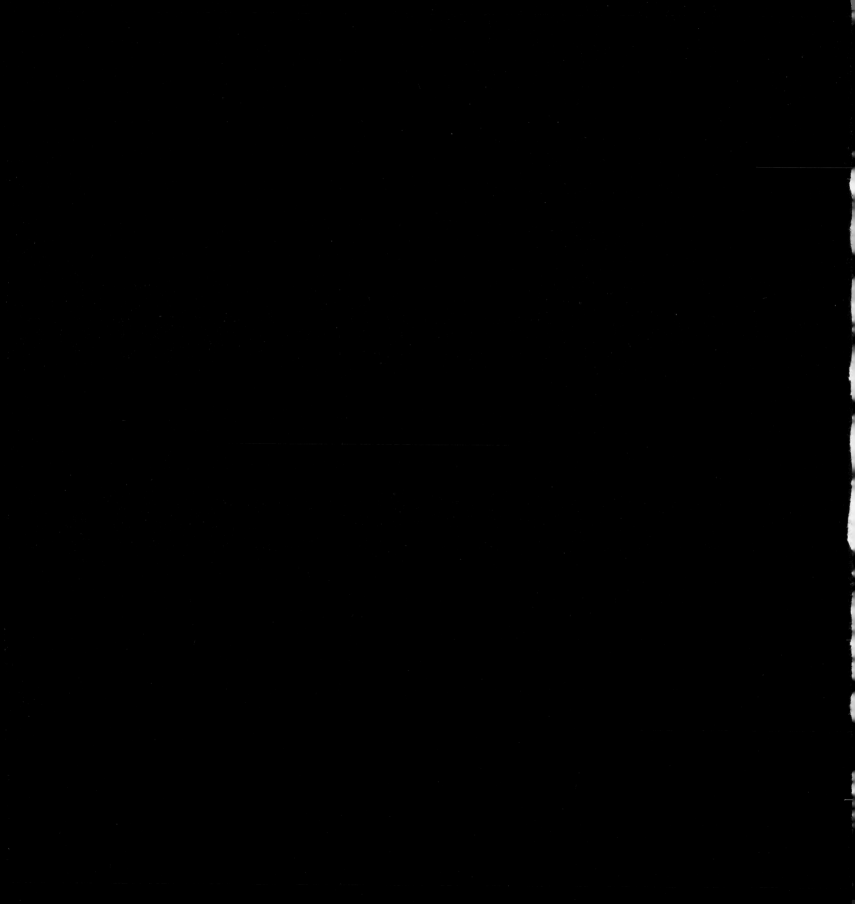

NORWAY

NATURAL BEAUTY

NORWAY

NATURAL BEAUTY

Ola Wakløv and Per Eide

Translated by William Mulholland

FONT FORLAG

TABLE OF CONTENTS

HISTORY OF NORWAY

From the Ice Age to the Bronze Age *(up to 500 BC)*

When the last Ice Age gradually released its grip around 14,000 years ago, parts of the Norwegian coast emerged from the vast layers of ice that had covered Northern Europe for several thousand years. The oldest definite traces of human presence in Norway were found at Blomvåg outside Bergen and have been dated to around 10,500 BC. The first influx of people to the country must be regarded against the background of the environmental changes at the end of the Ice Age. The steppe and tundra areas on the European continent were covered by forests then, and the reindeer flocks migrated northward. Some families of hunters followed the reindeer, eventually coming to an inviting Norwegian skerry landscape with ample supplies of fish, marine animals and birds. As early as around 9,300 BC some families had reached as far as Magerøya at the North Cape in Finnmark.

The first agriculture came to the districts surrounding the Oslo Fjord around 4000 BC, about 5000 years after it had first been developed in the Middle East. The old hunter population acquired knowledge of cattle and livestock farming through contacts with farmers farther south in Scandinavia, and as time passed they began to cultivate grain crops and keep cattle, sheep, goats and pigs. This development may be linked to the fact that the *battle axe people* migrated into the country. They have received their name after the beautifully carved stone axes that have been found in their graves, and it may have been these people who brought the Indo-European language north with them.

The Bronze Age (1800 – 500 BC) was a period with considerable changes in agriculture and lifestyle. The farmers settled down to a greater extent and began to build permanent farming facilities, especially in the areas around the Oslo Fjord, at Lake Mjøsa, in Jæren on the southwestern tip of the country and further north in Trøndelag. Large grave sites and finds of jewellery and ornaments from this period bear witness to an increasing standard of life and the beginnings of separation into social classes. The magnificent bronze objects belonged first and foremost to a rich upper class of chieftains who had settled in the best agricultural districts. Most people continued to use stone, bone and wood for both weapons and tools. For them it was probably more important that workhorses came into use and that the women learned how to spin and weave. A primary source of our knowledge of the Bronze Age period is the magnificent rock drawings which were intended to ensure fertility in the fields and among animals and people. Pictures of ritual processions with strong erotic elements provide us with mysterious glimpses of the religious world of these people. In the Bronze Age there existed a special catching culture which extended from Jemtland to the Varanger Fjord, and which is clearly distinct from the agricultural culture along the Norwegian coast. Weapons and tools of bronze after these hunters have been found which have much in common with Finnish and Russian finds. It is possible they spoke a Finnish-Ugrian language and were the forefathers of the Sami people. Not before around the birth of Christ do we find the first sure signs of Sami settlement. Then the Sami are also mentioned by the Roman historian Tacitus.

The Iron Age and chieftains' power (500 BC to 800 AD)

In the centuries prior to the birth of Christ the climate of Norway became colder and damper, until the weather was quite similar to what we have today. The heat-loving deciduous forests were gradually replaced by fir, birch and spruce. Farmers had to build more buildings that could provide heat and shelter to both people and animals, thus they became even more tied to the areas that had been core agricultural districts since the Bronze Age. At the same time knowledge of iron spread from the Celts in the south. The new metal was derived from ore that was readily available in marshes, and most people were able to acquire weapons and tools of iron. This made it easier to till the land; crops became more bountiful, the population rose, and land was cleared for more and more farms.

On the oldest Iron Age farms several generations lived under the same roof. Such an extended family was called a *clan*, and this gave security and protection to all who belonged to it. When there were conflicts between the clans in a settlement, all free men met at the *ting* (a legislative and judicial assembly), on a sacred place where the use of force was forbidden. Grave relics from the period after the birth of Christ clearly show that the clans from the biggest farms became richer and gained greater influence in a number of areas, and in the centuries leading to the Viking period an aristocracy of chieftains emerged. Today we find traces of such chieftain's power bases in geographical names such as Rogaland and Ringerike. The chieftains also functioned as priests when sacrificial feasts were held for gods such as Njord and Freia. In times of unrest they headed the defence forces, and the most powerful among them acquired a body of professional soldiers, a so-called *hird*. The chieftains had great influence in the community, and they also played a major role when trading missions were to be organized. Goods were bartered freely between north and south during this period, and in the graves of the period's more affluent farmers Roman bronze pots, gold ornaments and glassware have been found. They developed their own writing symbols, the *runes*, from the Latin alphabet, and they also utilized the Romans' system of weights.

During the turbulent migratory period of the Germanic tribes from 400 to 550 BC the chieftains gained greater power and authority to lead the defence of the settlements, and a number of fortifications were built to ward off foreign tribes that had come to the country after the collapse of the Western Roman Empire. The aristocratic chieftains' power bases that evolved throughout the Iron Age were an organizational prerequisite for expansion from the Nordic countries in the Viking period. Their highly developed shipbuilding expertise, good iron weapons and a religion that eulogized the warrior ideal, were other important background factors. However, Norwegian expansion was also a result of a lack of land and new market demands. In the rest of Europe there was a great demand for iron, fur clothing, reindeer skin, walrus teeth, seal skin and down.

The Viking period and consolidation of the nation (800 – 1030)

The attack on the Lindisfarne monastery on the east coast of Northern England in the year 793 is regarded by many as the beginning of the Viking period. The first Viking raids from Norway were aimed at the British Isles, Iceland and Greenland. But the Viking missions were often joint Nordic expeditions, and Norwegians also took part in the expansion eastward and southward along with Danes and Swedes. More and more emphasis is being placed on the fact that the Vikings were not just robbers and murderers but also skilled craftsmen, traders, shipbuilders, sailors and explorers. They discovered Iceland at the end of the 9th century, and this island became a centre for the Norse saga literature. The foremost of the Norwegian dominion's own authors was

In Norse mythology Yggdrasil spreads its branches over the whole world, and at one of the roots of the tree there is a well that gives wisdom and understanding. The god of war, Odin, gave one of his eyes to its guardian, Mime, for the right to draw from the well. A wood sculpture from Gamlebyen (the Old Town), Oslo.

Snorre Sturlason writes that the Viking king Halvdan the Black, who was the father of Harald Fair Hair, drowned when he fell through the ice at Randsfjorden with his horse and sled. Chieftains from Romerike, Vestfold and Hedmark all wanted to take his corpse with them to place it in a burial mound, and they agreed to divide the body, so that all four regions got their Halvdan's Mound. According to tradition it is Halvdan's head that lies in the majestic burial mound from the year 860 at Hole in Buskerud.

the Icelander Snorre Sturlason (1179–1241), whose sagas of the kings are still an important source for historians. Here, among other things, we are told that the Vikings settled in Greenland in the 980s under the leadership of Eirik the Red from Rogaland. Around the year 1000 Eirik's son Leiv led an expedition along the coast of North America. They spent the winter at the north edge of Newfoundland, and the remains of this settlement were excavated in the 1960s by a group of archaeologists led by Anne Stine and Helge Ingstad.

It was probably the desire to safeguard their own trading interests that was the motive force behind Harald Fairhair's attempt to be recognized as king of the whole nation around the year 900. According to Snorre, Harald belonged to the powerful Yngling clan from Vestfold, and he had financial interests in Skiringssal, the greatest trading centre in Norway in the 9th century. He was therefore interested in securing the sea-lane along the Norwegian coast against Viking attack, and entered into an alliance with chieftains in Møre and in Trøndelag to beat off the pirates in West Norway. Harald annexed the farms of affluent farmers who refused to recognize him as monarch of the realm, and these confiscated landed properties laid the foundation for the Norwegian royal estate in the Middle Ages. At the end of the 9th century Harald won a decisive battle at Hafrsfjord in Rogaland.

Harald's son, Håkon the Good, extended this power base by establishing *lagtingene*, which were regional courts consisting of royal appointees sent from the local courts within a region. Thereafter he got the regional courts to agree to establish a naval defence scheme, *leidangen*, where the law stipulated that farmers were to supply longships with crew and equipment for bi-monthly service periods. The ships stood under royal command and were to be called upon with the help of signal fires. The creation of the regional courts and naval defence scheme shows that the farmers regarded themselves as being well served by a nationwide kingdom that assured them of law and order and protection against external enemies. As the 10th century progressed the royal ombudsmen were given more and more duties. They were responsible for appointing representatives to the regional courts and for administering the naval defence scheme. In addition they managed the royal palaces, had responsibility for law and order and collected goods and fines from the farmers.

Harald Hairfair's descendents were constantly in conflict with Danish kings who claimed hegemony in Norway. They collaborated with the earls of Lade in Trøndelag, which in the decades around the year 1000 were vassals of the Danish king. Many Norwegian chieftains disliked the fact that the Hairfair kings made incursions into their old areas of power, and several of them were particularly sceptical about the attempts to introduce Christianity. Many chieftains believed that the new religion would take their positions as religious leaders and clan chiefs from them. It was therefore not difficult for the Danish king, Knut the Powerful, to find allies. The Hairfair kings Olav Tryggvason and Olav Haraldsson (the saint) were both vanquished by Dano-Norwegian alliances, and after the fall of Olav Haraldsson at Stiklestad in 1030 it looked as if the Hairfair dynasty had lost the battle for royal power in Norway.

The Middle Ages (1030 – 1319)

The Danish king's illegitimate son, ten-year-old Svein Alfivason, became king of Norway after Olav's fall. However the Danish rule brought famine and repressive taxation with it, and Svein soon gained a bad reputation. In the meanwhile rumours also arose that a number of miracles had taken place where Olav had been secretly buried by the Nidelva river, and one year after the king's death his corpse was dug up in view of the foremost persons in the country. Legend has it that he was just as handsome as when he had been buried, and that his hair and beard had continued to grow. Olav was elevated to the status of patron saint; that is how the kings of Norway for all time to come would be linked to God, and Olav's descendents were granted a special right to the throne of Norway. In 1034 Danish rule had become so unpopular that one of Saint Olav's slayers from Stiklestad went to Gardarike, a kingdom in Russia, to bring home his eleven-year-old son Magnus. The year after he came to Norway and named himself king, and Svein left the country without offering resistance.

The hundred years that followed were characterized by peace and growth. The population grew quickly, and now the first cities also emerged, with Nidaros, Oslo, Borg, Tunsberg and Bergen as the most important ones. However, the large majority of the inhabitants were still linked to the agricultural community. In the Viking period the farmers owned their farms, but by around 1300 much of the land had changed owner. The majority of the farmers had become tenant farmers under the Church, king or nobility, who now owned altogether 70 per cent of the land. There were a number of reasons for the transition to the tenant farmer system. Firstly, the kings during the 10th and 11th centuries confiscated land from their opponents. Secondly, new settlers automatically became tenant farmers under the Crown. Further, the strong growth in population led to a scarcity of resources. Farms were divided, and farmers might become debtors, so that they were forced to sell all or parts of their farms. Many also gave land to the Church so that the priests would pray for them, and such religious gifts contributed to making the Church the country's biggest landowner. Nevertheless, Norwegian tenant farmers retained their position as legally free farmers throughout the Middle Ages.

King Sigurd Jorsalfar's death in 1130 marks the inception of the so-called civil war period. The system of succession to the throne was so vague that all the sons of kings, both legitimate and illegitimate, could claim the right to become king. A number of pretenders to the throne strug-gled for power, some of them small children, and behind them stood powerful chieftains from various regions. Norway was still not a close-knit political unit, and the Church was still the only well-developed organization in the country. During the tumultuous period of the civil war the Church increased its power, and in 1152 a special Norwegian ecclesiastical province with an archdiocese in Nidaros was established. Under Archbishop Øystein it attempted to create a kingdom that it could form and control. Foremost in the fight against the Church stood Sverre, the leader of a flock of rebels called *birkebeinerne* (the Birch Legs). He was excommunicated by the Pope, and never managed to become ruler of the whole country. Not until 1217 was the country again unified under one king, Håkon Håkonsson, Sverre's grandson. He sought peace with the Church, and it was during his long period of rule in the 13th century that the "Old Norwegian Golden Age" began.

In the 13th century the king of Norway ruled over more land than ever before, and both Iceland and Greenland came under Norwegian rule. The strength of the kingdom also showed itself in the administration of the country. King Magnus Lagabøte had a law encompassing the whole of Norway prepared, *Landsloven*. The country was divided into 50 administrative districts, the king's chancery grew forth, and Norway was now a political unit. During the Golden Age literary life also flourished. Elements from French novels and tales of adventure from the East blended with the native Norwegian genres, and the country gradually acquired its own national literature. We can also see traces of this period in a number of Norwegian cities. The Archbishop's Palace was erected next to the Nidaros Cathedral, Håkon's Hall was built in Bergen and around 1300 Akershus Fortress in Oslo was completed in its original form.

The Norwegian dominion had a secure position around 1300, but the royal policy on marriage was creating anxiety. King Håkon V Magnusson, who ruled the country at the beginning of the 14th century, did not have a son. He had

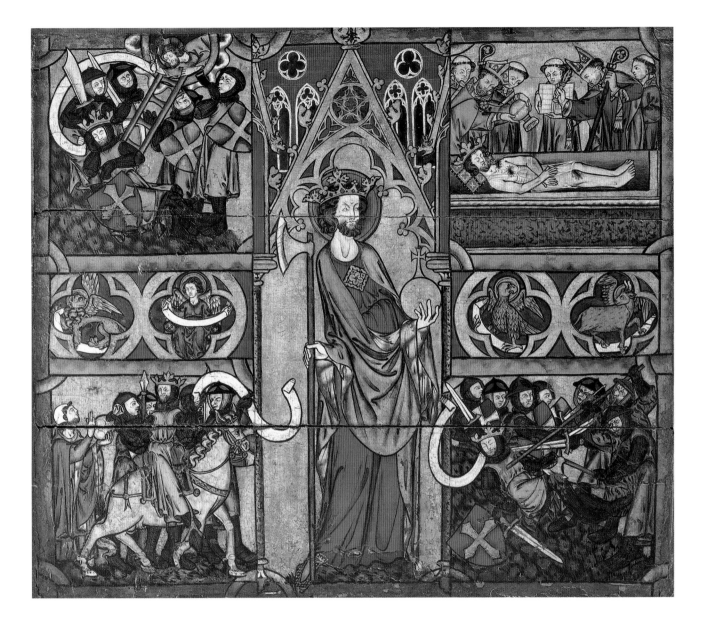

Saint Olav's life and death are depicted in this magnificent altar from the 14TH century. It originally comes from Haltdalen Stave Church in Trøndelag, but after the Reformation in 1537 it was sent to Denmark. In connection with the Saint Olav Jubilee in 1930 it was returned to Norway, and is now to be found in the Nidaros Cathedral in Trondheim.

According to ancient legend the Black Death, or the Great Slayer of Men as it was most often called, went the rounds as a female character called Pesta. In the 19TH century the artist Theodor Kittelsen (1857–1914) created the poetic depiction *The Black Death,* a gloomy, original and imaginative work that holds a special place in Norwegian literature.

a daughter by the daughter of a German count, and he married her off to the Swedish Duke Erik of Södermanland. She had a son, Magnus, by him. In 1319 the Hairfair family died out on the male side, and Norway was faced with an uncertain future.

Union, depopulation and the Reformation
(1319 – 1537)

After the death of Håkon V the three-year-old Magnus Erikson inherited the throne of Norway. In the same year he was also chosen to be king of Sweden, so that both countries entered into a dynastic union. In Norway the state council was compelled to rule in collaboration with the king's mother, Ingebjørg, but when she attempted to subjugate the Danish region of Skåne, the council expelled her from the national government. When Magnus came of age he continued his mother's policy, but now both state councils intervened. He was deposed and it was decided that his two sons would each be given a throne when they came of age. Thus we see that the state council had grown forth as an independent and powerful governing body, and it now attempted to repair the damage the joint kingship had caused. However, far graver disasters were about to befall Norway.

It was probably an English ship that brought the bubonic plague to Norway in the summer of 1349, and in the course of the autumn and winter a third of the population was wiped out. Around 1400 the population was halved as new local plagues struck, and not until after 1500 did the population figures begin to rise again. Even before the plague arrived, the country was enmeshed in a crisis concerning resources. The increase in population had led to a run on farms, the soil had been ravaged and food resources had diminished. However, after 1349 there was plenty of land available, and people moved to the richest and best farming areas. It was difficult for the big landowners to lease out their land, it was cheaper to rent land, and the burden of taxation fell. The lack of labour caused many farming families to change from agriculture to livestock farming. Land that had been neglected was used as pastureland, and people ate more protein-rich food than previously.

The reduced state income undermined the Norwegian governmental system. The farming community took over more of the medieval state's functions, and the farmers began to govern themselves in a way they had not done for a long time. The lesser Norwegian nobility, which had been poor and few in number compared to its peers in the neighbouring countries, was further reduced in power and importance. The more exalted nobility were better off, since a king with reduced powers gave them greater leeway, but now Swedes and Danes married into Norwegian noble families. The Church was the country's biggest landowner, and it managed better than the king and nobility. People feared death more than ever, so they gave land to the Church to save their own souls. The archbishop of Nidaros was now Norway's most powerful man and the obvious choice as leader of the state council.

In this way Norway became a political power vacuum paving the way for expansion from its neighbours, notably Denmark. The population of Sweden and Denmark was greater than that of Norway, and their agricultural areas were many times bigger. In the 14th and 15th centuries the Hanseatic Union took over control of Norwegian foreign trade, and Bergen became a centre for the import of grain and export of dried fish. In all of the Nordic countries anxiety about the Germans' economic and political progress was growing, and it is against this background we must view the Kalmar Union.

After the dynastic union with Sweden was dissolved, King Håkon VI married the Danish king's daughter, Margaret. This created a problematic relationship with Sweden and saw the inception of a dynastic struggle for power in the Nordic countries. Håkon and Margaret had one son, Olav. He was chosen to be Danish king in 1375, and also inherited the throne of Norway upon his father's death in 1380. Thus Denmark and Norway formed a union, something that would last right up to 1814. When Olav died Margaret managed to put her under-age relative, Erik of Pommern, on the throne. Thereafter she attacked Sweden, and in 1397 the union between the three Nordic states was sealed at Kalmar. Erik of Pommern was crowned king of the Nordic states, and Margaret herself ruled the three states with a firm hand.

Her policy was aimed at strengthening royal power and weakening the state councils. Sweden and Norway were to be subordinated to the main country, Denmark. Erik of Pommern carried Margaret's anti-German policy further, which resulted in war both with German princes and with the Hanseatics. Bergen was attacked and plundered, and the Norwegian naval defence force was routed by the Hanseatics' war vessels. The German blockade and heavy taxes were an onerous burden on Norway, and both in Norway and in Sweden rural rebellions broke out. The higher Swedish nobility exploited this turbulent situation to withdraw the country from the union, but the Norwegian state council was too weak. It proved impossible to restore a separate Norwegian kingdom.

The treaty of union of 1450 stated that Denmark and Norway were to be under one king for all time. Now Norway remained standing outside the centre of events, but in 1523 a powerful politician took the archbishop's seat in Nidaros. Olav Engelbrektsson realized that Luther's teachings were a threat to the Catholic Church in Norway. As archbishop and head of the state council he made every effort to keep the country free from "the Lutheran poison". But Olav failed, and in the spring of 1537 Danish forces arrived in Norway. Olav fled, and the Evangelical Lutheran State Church was introduced. The king took over all the Church's property, and the last defenders of Norway's independence, the Catholic Church and the state council, were gone.

Norway in the union with Denmark *(1537 – 1814)*

After the downfall of the Catholic Church the sparse Norwegian nobility was too weak to maintain the independence of the nation. The king ruled Norway from Copenhagen along with his Danish state counsellors, and it was he – not the Pope in Rome – who was head of the Church. However, even though the written language became Danish, the Norwegian spoken language and customs lived on, and the sources show that the inhabitants of Norway felt they were *Norwegians*.

The Danish king who has left the deepest impression on Norway is Christian IV. He founded Kristiansand, built a number of fortresses and secured control of the northern regions of Norway. He developed the Norwegian mining industry, revised Magnus Lagabøte's national law from 1276 and laid the foundation for a separate Norwegian army in 1628. However, his political ambitions abroad, and the wars of the first half of the 17th century, meant that Norway had to relinquish both Jemtland and Herjedalen to Sweden.

When Frederik III took absolute power in 1660, the tribute to the succession in Norway was merely a formality, but the ceremony says much about the difference between Danish and Norwegian farmers at that time. At the tribute to the succession in Denmark only a handful of farmers were present, while at the tribute in Christiania 408 farmers out of 543 representatives of the national assembly attended. Norwegian farmers were among the freest in Europe.

Between 1500 and 1800 the population increased from 150,000 to nearly 900,000, and the main reason for this was that the attacks of plague came to an end. Nine out of ten Norwegians belonged to the peasant class, which was the backbone of Norwegian society throughout the period. During the period of absolute monarchy the opposite of what we saw in the Middle Ages occurred: Now Norwegian farmers were gradually becoming owner-occupiers – they were purchasing the right of ownership to the land they

CHRISTIAN IV (1577–1648) WAS THE DANISH KING WHO PLAYED THE MOST IMPORTANT ROLE IN NORWAY. HE WAS BARELY 11 YEARS OLD WHEN HIS FATHER DIED, AND FORMALLY SPEAKING HE REIGNED FOR 60 YEARS. THE PICTURE WAS PAINTED BY PIETER ISAACSZ SHORTLY AFTER THE KALMAR WAR (1611–1613).

were already working. The king and the bourgeoisie sold land and invested the capital thus released in other activities. Only in North Norway did the landowners abstain from this due to the hunting and fishing rights which were linked to the farms, and in time many fishermen-farmers fell hopelessly in debt to merchants in Bergen and Trondheim.

From the 16th century the timber trade evolved into a primary industry. The economic expansion in Western Europe led to a great demand for timber for ships and house-building. However, later in the 17th century the farmers were pushed out of the most profitable sectors within the timber trade: sawmills and sales. The state gave a small group of citizens a monopoly of such business, and a powerful trade patriciate came to dominate the bourgeoisie in those cities that exported timber. But the mining sector too influenced the farming community. Farmers who lived in the proximity of mines and works had to supply wood and charcoal for a miserable remuneration.

Toward the end of the 18th century the bonds between Denmark and Norway were strong. Economically and culturally government officials and the citizenry were linked to Denmark, and Norwegian farmers were confident that the king in Copenhagen would protect them if they were subjected to improper treatment by government officials. Nevertheless, Norwegian self-awareness had grown forth in the farming community and in the cultural elite. It was the farmers who paid taxes and who made up the Norwegian army, and the customs revenues from fishing, timber and mining streamed into the king's treasury in Copenhagen.

1814 – Independence and a new union

The Napoleonic Wars raged in Europe from 1792 right up to 1814. Denmark-Norway was on France's side, for Norway this meant blockade and years of deprivation, and dissatisfaction with the unitary state policy increased.

In autumn 1813 the Danish heir presumptive Christian Frederik came to Norway as vice-regent. On behalf of the king he was to watch over the double monarchy and safeguard Norway as a Danish area. However after the Treaty of Kiel in January 1814 a dramatic situation arose: Since Denmark had been on the loosing side in The Napoleonic wars, Norway was awarded to the king of Sweden, and the 438-year-old long union between Norway and Denmark was therefore over. In Norway the heir presumptive was surrounded by a loyal state administration, a loyal bourgeoisie and farmers loyal to the king who constituted the backbone of the Norwegian army. However, even though he was popular, his claim as rightful heir to the throne of Norway was rejected by a meeting of prominent men at Eidsvoll. The people had to have an opportunity to state their opinion. The result was that an elected, broadly composed national assembly met at Eidsvoll in April to create a constitution. On 17 May 1814 the Constitution was ratified and Christian Frederik chosen to be constitutional king. The period of absolute monarchy was irrevocably at an end.

The Constitution was particularly inspired by the French one from 1791, and the sovereignty of the people was a fundamental principle. A distinction was made between the legislative, executive and judicial power, but the king was given a strong position in relation to the popularly elected parliament, the *Storting*. The Constitution was a compromise between absolute monarchy and democracy, and the rules concerning the right to vote were liberal viewed with contemporary eyes, as almost half of all men over the age of 25 were given the right to vote.

By the late spring of 1814 Napoleon had been crushed, and the Swedish crown prince Carl Johan was able to implement the provisions of the Treaty of Kiel. The great powers refused to recognize an independent Norway. They suspected a double game on the part of Denmark aimed at restoring the Dano-Norwegian double monarchy. At the end of July Carl Johan entered southern Norway with 40 –

The Norwegian Constitution was signed by 112 elected representatives in the National Assembly at Eidsvoll 17 May 1814. Today Oscar Wergeland's painting hangs behind the rostrum of the Storting in Oslo.

50,000 battle-hardened soldiers. The Norwegian army consisted of 30,000 poorly-trained and ill-equipped men, and the war was short-lived.

On 4 November 1814 Carl XIII of Sweden was chosen to be king of Norway after a revision of the Constitution. The main principles from Eidsvoll remained standing. Carl Johan accepted the situation, but he did not regard the Constitution as a permanent and unchangeable document.

Norway from 1814 to 1905

To a great extent Norway had been cut of from cultural impulses for more than 400 years, but the absence of European fine arts had also strengthened and conserved the Norwegian folk art. It was still the case that only a minority of Norwegians lived in the cities; most people were self-sufficient and had to rely on their own creative abilities, in aesthetic pursuits too. Nevertheless, or perhaps precisely because of this, not many decades would pass before the country had fostered writers, artists and composers such as Henrik Ibsen, Knut Hamsun, Edvard Munch and Edvard Grieg.

Although the blockades of the Napoleonic Wars had now been raised, Norway was struck by an economic crisis. This was caused by a combination of trade restrictions on timber and galloping inflation. The crisis primarily affected the rich bourgeoisie and the state treasury, while farmers generally got by on what they produced on their farms. As far as political power was concerned the situation was largely the opposite. In the decades following 1814 state officials played a key role. They were alone in having ministerial positions; they dominated the Storting and controlled the military and civil administration.

It was the farmers in particular who were growing dissatisfied, and when the Executive Committee Acts, which ordered the establishment of popularly elected municipal councils, were passed in 1837, the farmers acquired greater influence in their local councils. In the 1860s a nationwide rural movement arose which gained a majority in the Storting. The farmers wanted to reduce state expenditures and formed an alliance with the total abstinence movement, Landsmål[1] advocates, lay Christians and urban radicals. Under the leadership of Johan Sverdrup this opposition attacked the governing bureaucracy. It demanded that the king should appoint ministers who were duty-bound to attend the meetings of the Storting and who were responsible to the national assembly. For a number of years the king refused to accept the demands of the opposition, but after a government composed of state officials was deposed through impeachment in 1884, he gave way and consented to appoint a new government with Johan Sverdrup as prime minister. For the first time a politician was appointed as head of government because he had a majority of the Storting's representatives behind him. Thus was parliamentary government introduced in Norway.

The conflict surrounding parliamentary government gave rise to the first political parties. The circle around Sverdrup formed Venstre (the Liberal Party), while the state officials and the bourgeoisie formed Høyre (the Conservative Party). A conflict concerning cultural policy soon led to a split in Venstre. The dissenters sought collaboration with Høyre, which quickly got rid of its links to officialdom and received increasing support from the middle class and well-to-do farmers.

Industrialization started in Christiania, Bergen and Trondheim in the 1840s. The period after 1850 was also an expansive time for shipping and a period of modernization in agriculture. However, the growth of industry and shipping was too modest to absorb all the crofters and farm workers that were no longer needed in the farming industry, and many emigrated to America. By 1915 approximately 750,000 Norwegians had travelled to the USA. Seen in relation to the population figures it was only Ireland that experienced greater emigration than Norway.

The labour movement grew forth in the 1880s, in hard conflict with employers and political authorities. Arbeider-

[1] Name of *nynorsk* (the New Norwegian language) prior to 1929.

ON THE 4TH OF JULY 1825 52 NORWEGIANS SAILED WESTWARD FROM STAVANGER WITH THE GOOD SHIP "RESTAURATIONEN", AND IN THE HUNDRED YEARS THAT FOLLOWED ABOUT 800,000 NORWEGIANS LEFT NORWAY TO SETTLE IN AMERICA. THE NORWEGIAN IMMIGRANTS BROUGHT A SOLIDLY ROOTED TRADITION OF COLLABORATION FROM THEIR LOCAL COMMUNITIES. THE PICTURE WAS TAKEN IN THE YEAR 1900 AND SHOWS THE BUILDING OF A BARN IN RAINY RIVER, MINNESOTA.

In connection with the Berlin Secession in 1902 Edvard Munch (1863–1944) exhibited *Vampire* and 21 other paintings from the 1890s under the name *The Frieze of Life*. Munch himself referred to the frieze as "a poem about love, anxiety and death", and stated that with these pictures he wished to "achieve an explanation of life and its meaning — ... [and] help others to see life clearly". This exhibition is regarded by many as Munch's commercial breakthrough.

partiet (the Labour Party) was founded in 1887, and received support from an increasing number of labour unions. The party oriented itself in a socialist direction, but did not obtain mass support before the 20th century.

The dynastic union between Norway and Sweden did not just lead to joint kingship, but also to a joint foreign service and defence and foreign policy. Norway had its own army, own state bureaucracy and own parliament, and the union led only to a small degree to economic integration between the countries. Nor did it strengthen the cultural ties, and a dawning Norwegian nationalism during the second half of the 19th century coincided with significant progress within the Norwegian artistic, industrial and scientific sectors. Not least did Fridtjof Nansen's polar expeditions provide an important stimulus to nationalistic feelings.

When parliamentary government was introduced in 1884, the Storting strengthened its position in relation to the king. In the 1890s Norway upgraded its armed forces, and when after long-drawn-out negotiations Sweden rejected Norway's demand for a separate consular service, a hard line was chosen. In spring 1905 the Storting passed an Act stipulating a separate Norwegian consular service. When the king refused to sign it, the government withdrew from office and the Storting declared that the union had been dissolved. Sweden demanded a referendum, but only 184 Norwegians said yes to a continued union. On a snowy November day in 1905 Prince Carl of Denmark came to Norway as King Haakon VII, after 80 per cent of the people had voted that Norway should be a kingdom. Norway could finally take its place among the independent states of Europe.

A free Norway (1905 – 1940)

Not before 1905 did industrialization and urbanization really pick up speed, and in 1916 industry was producing almost twice as much as in 1905. The dissolution of the

KING HAAKON VII COMES TO NORWAY AS NORWEGIAN KING 25 NOVEMBER 1905, AND IS WELCOMED AT THE DOCKSIDE IN KRISTIANIA (OSLO) BY PRIME MINISTER CHRISTIAN MICHELSEN. ON THE KING'S ARM SITS HIS SON, CROWN PRINCE OLAV, WHO WAS CONSTITUTED AS PRINCE REGENT IN CONNECTION WITH HIS FATHER'S ILLNESS IN 1955, AND ACCEDED TO THE THRONE UPON HAAKON'S DEATH IN 1957. OLAV V WAS HEAD OF STATE IN NORWAY UNTIL HIS DEATH IN 1991.

union created optimism and the desire to work. Hydro-electric power supplied industry with plentiful, cheap electricity, and the development of industrial production led to increased demand for Norwegian goods. Foreign investments in trade and industry grew strongly, something which also caused anxiety in the young nation. Who should own Norwegian waterfalls, forests and mines? In 1909 and in 1917 the Storting passed laws that restricted the freedom of action of foreign capital interests. The so-called licensing laws obliged foreigners to apply to the government for permission to exploit Norwegian natural resources.

The period after 1900 was characterized by modernization of the traditional business sectors. In agriculture mechanization continued, and more and more fishermen got motorized boats with drift nets or seines. After the turn of the century whaling began in the Antarctic Ocean. However, at the same time the dark side of industrial society became more evident. New laws regarding factory inspection, accident insurance and the 10-hour working day were passed to correct the worst conditions. However, the welfare state was still far in the future.

In the period between 1906 and 1920 Venstre was the leading political party with Gunnar Knudsen as its leader. This party stood at the vanguard concerning extension of the right to vote, and in 1913 women were given a general right to vote at elections to the Storting. Men had had this right since 1898.

As an independent state Norway chose to adopt a neutral foreign policy. However, when the First World War broke out in the summer of 1914, Norway's sympathies in relation to Britain became clearly evident. Soon German U-boats were attacking Norwegian merchant ships, and the government responded by putting most of the merchant fleet at the disposal of the British. In return Norway received the promise of oil and coal supplies. A total of over 2000 seamen lost their lives, and about 800 ships were lost. The fact that Norway was not drawn directly into the war is due not least to the fact that both blocks gained from Norwegian neutrality. Norway was a weak military power and neither of the parties wished to tie up their own troops on Norwegian soil. The war economy exacerbated class conflicts in Norway. Speculators were raking in enormous profits on the stock market, whereas most people were being hard hit by inflation and the scarcity of wares. In this situation the labour movement was radicalized, while the fear of socialism increased among the bourgeoisie.

As early as in 1918 radicals took over control of the Norwegian Labour Party. They put revolution on the agenda and registered the party in the Comintern. This change

of course created division, and a social-democratic opposition broke out in 1921. The Communists formed their own party two years later, when the Labour Party withdrew from the Communist International, but the social democrats did not rejoin the party before 1927. The party division contributed to the combative strength of the union movement being weakened and membership numbers fell dramatically. The labour movement also faced opposition in the form of new laws that introduced compulsory arbitration in wage conflicts and protected strike-breakers.

Between 1917 and 1935 the political situation was unstable. In the 1920s Høyre and Venstre took turns being in government, while Bondepartiet (the Farmers' Party) had this responsibility at the beginning of the 1930s. Political instability, times of crisis and fear of the labour movement created an atmosphere conducive to the rise of extreme right-wing movements. The semi-military organization "Samfunnsvernet" (Societal Protection) received support from both conservative governments and powerful capitalist interests. This "white guard" was to be mobilized if the establishment was threatened. The nationalist organization "Fedrelandslaget" (the Fatherland Association), with about 100,000 members, was opposed to parliamentary democracy and stood forth with clear fascist sympathies. However, Norway got a special fascist party in 1933, when Vidkun Quisling founded Nasjonal Samling (National Unification). But the party received little support, and by the outbreak of war in 1940 it had been reduced to an isolated sect.

The international post-war crisis affected Norway extra hard because of the authorities' monetary policy. The aim was to increase the value of the Norwegian crown in relation to the pound. In order to combat inflation the government reduced the quantity of money. This meant that the capitalists invested less, so growth slowed accordingly. Since the price of goods was falling, it became more difficult for enterprises, farmers and fishermen to pay back their debts. Banks and businesses went bankrupt, and a number of farms had to

Fridtjof Nansen (1861–1930) was a zoologist, polar researcher and politician. He crossed Greenland on skis in 1888, and led the Fram expedition to the Arctic five years later. After the First World War he worked tirelessly to improve the situation of prisoners of war and refugees in Russia and South eastern Europe. He introduced the Nansen Passport for stateless persons, and was honoured with the Nobel Peace Prize in 1922 for his unique humanitarian contribution.

be sold at auction. Unemployment and social deprivation led to hopelessness and resentment in broad strata of society.

At the beginning of the 1930s the Labour Party developed a crisis management programme inspired by the British economist J.M. Keynes. They won the election of 1933 with this programme and then formed a minority government which remained in power until 1945. With alternating support from the Farmers' Party and Liberal Party the Nygaardsvold government implemented a number of important policies. Higher direct and indirect taxes gave the state greater revenues, which were used to alleviate the crisis. New laws regarding old age pensions, unemployment benefit and worker protection bear witness to a new atmosphere of cooperation in politics. One part of the basis for cooperation was laid in 1935, when the national organizations in the employment sector, LO (Norwegian Federation of Trade Unions) and NAF (Norwegian Confederation of Employers), agreed to establish a national collective agreement, the Basic Agreement. This ensured workers the right to organize and stipulated guidelines for negotiations on wages and working conditions.

When Norway became a member of the League of Nations in 1920, it was feared that this could undermine its policy of neutrality and draw the country into conflicts between the great powers. However, the risk of new wars seemed small, and the business sector was critical of isolationist policy. Thus, no more critical questions about membership were raised before the end of the 1930s. When the danger of war increased, Norway declared itself exempt from any duty to impose sanctions and returned to its old policy of neutrality.

In Norway too imperialistic attitudes made their mark on foreign policy. Norwegian expansion was directed at areas of particular interest to fishermen and other catchers. In 1925 the great powers accepted that Norway was given sovereignty over Svalbard, and some years later Norway also annexed Bouvet Island and Peter I's Island in the Antarctic Ocean. At the beginning of the 1930s the government gave its support to fishermen and catchers from Western Norway occupying Eastern Greenland. Denmark had this conflict taken up by the International Court of Justice at the Hague, whereupon Norwegian Arctic imperialism suffered its greatest defeat.

Upgrading the Norwegian armed forces had low priority before 1940. The danger of attack was regarded as little, and Norway's possibility of repulsing an attack by a great power was in any event regarded as small. Experience from the First World War indicated that the country would be able to stay out of new wars. Thus, surprise and confusion characterized people's reactions when Germany launched its attack on 9 April 1940.

War and occupation (1940 – 1945)

In September 1939 Germany attacked Poland, and as Britain and France stood on the side of Poland, the Second World War was in progress. Only a few months later both the Western powers and Germany were engaged in military operations against the Nordic countries. The French were interested in engaging Hitler in the north to ease the pressure on their own borders, but Britain viewed with increasing anxiety the fact that Germany was exploiting Norwegian waters to its own advantage. The need to stop the Swedish export of iron ore to the German war industry, and at the same time help the Finns in the Winter War, was also a major motive force behind British planning.

The German naval command wished to have bases along the Norwegian coast, but control over Norway also suited Hitler's vision of a Greater German Nazi Europe confronting the Communist Soviet Union. In the course of the morning hours of 9 April 1940 the Germans occupied their objectives along the coast without meeting significant resistance. However, the attempt to establish an indirect government along Danish lines was not successful. Such a scheme had to be given up because the members of the Norwegian government and the royal family avoided capture.

Despite the odds the Nygaardsvold government chose to take up arms. Moreover, a negotiated solution with the Germans was unthinkable after Quisling staged a coup d'état, and Hitler demanded that the king should appoint the Norwegian Nazi leader as prime minister. The Norwegian government had also staked its trust in the allies, who promised to come to the rescue. However the efforts by the soldiers of the Western allies were to little avail, and in June 1940 the king and members of the government sailed to Britain. From there they continued the struggle with the help of the merchant fleet and newly-organized military detachments, and the untiring efforts of King Haakon and Crown Prince Olav gave the government extra authority.

The government installed by the Germans was a military dictatorship led by *Reichskommissar* Josef Terboven. Norway became an important base in the Battle of the Atlantic and in the campaign against the Soviet Union, and in addition the German war machine availed itself generously of the country's resources, especially metals and fish products.

WHEN SOVIET TROOPS ADVANCED INTO EAST FINNMARK, THEY WERE HAILED AS LIBERATORS. IN THIS HISTORIC PICTURE FROM 1945 RUSSIAN SOLDIERS MEET CIVILIANS WHO HAD HIDDEN IN AN ORE MINE IN BJØRNEVATN.

With the support of Quisling the Germans wished to implement a National Socialist reform of Norwegian society. The Norwegian Nazis tried to gain control over sports, education, the Church and societal organizations, and began recruitment of Norwegian youth to front-line service for the Germans. This led to the growth of a broad civil resistance movement, but it was never allowed to participate in an allied invasion. In May 1945 the Germans conceded defeat after first having laid fiery waste to the whole of Finnmark and Nord-Troms as they retreated from advancing Soviet troops. A comprehensive courtroom showdown with Nazis and war criminals marked the end of five years of war. Vidkun Quisling and 24 others were executed. Once again Norway was free.

From liberation to the Common Market conflict
(1945 – 1972)

After liberation all the political parties stood behind a joint programme that prioritized economic growth, social security and an increasing standard of life. Right up to the end of the 1960s the country was characterized by social stability. This rested on the community spirit from the period of occupation, the work of reconstruction and the Cold War. The country reaped the benefits of the boom in the international economy, there was no industrial unrest and unemployment was a thing of the past.

This stability was reinforced by the political willingness to compromise in the Labour Party and its prime minister, Einar Gerhardsen. The Party now threw itself into the struggle to capture the votes of white-collar workers; they pigeon-holed core radical issues and stayed in power right up to the mid-1960s. When the centre-right parties took over responsibility for government in 1965, this did not lead to any significant change in course.

In the first years after liberation Norway collaborated with Britain and the USA, and trusted that the new global organization, the UN, would ensure peace. At the same time everyone agreed that the Norwegian armed forces must be strengthened. However, when the differences between East and West increased, Norway turned down a proposal for Nordic collaboration and joined NATO in 1949. In order to placate the Soviet Union the government issued the so-called base declaration, which prohibited the permanent stationing of foreign troop on Norwegian soil in peacetime.

In the 1950s Norway prioritized collaboration with Britain and the USA rather than with the Nordic countries and Europe. The attempts to establish a Nordic customs union were rejected by Norway, and not before the 1960s, when the country became a member of EFTA, did trade and industry have to accustom itself to increasing international competition.

Despite the political stability, the first decades after the war were not only characterized by harmony. The Communists protested against the Labour Party's NATO line and domestic right-wing policies, a criticism that was continued by the Socialist People's Party from 1961. The private business sector managed to prevent new regulatory

IN SPRING 1947 THOR HEYERDAHL (1914–2002) AND HIS CREW SAILED ACROSS THE PACIFIC OCEAN WITH THE "KON-TIKI", A COPY OF AN OLD PERUVIAN BALSA RAFT.

legislation, and adherents of the Christian People's Party launched harsh attacks on the labour movement's views on religious education, sexual morals and abortion.

Rationing of most consumer goods was phased out around 1950, but not before the 1960s was the range of available goods on a par with Norway's neighbouring countries. However, the superfluity of goods created new problems, and some sections of the youthful populace rebelled against their parents' materialism. Dissatisfaction with the authoritarian educational system and the USA-friendly for-

eign policy grew among students and school pupils. Increasing pollution and senseless use of resources laid the basis for an environmental movement. The radical students and environmentalists joined the active struggle against Norwegian membership of the EEC, and they were supported by people from the left and from the farmers' organizations, fishermen, lay Christians and New Norwegian adherents. This alliance aimed a serious blow at the country's economic and political élite when it won the referendum in 1972.

FEW MATTERS OF FOREIGN POLICY HAVE DIVIDED THE NORWEGIAN POPULATION MORE THAN THE QUESTION OF MEMBERSHIP OF THE EU. IN 1973 A SMALL MAJORITY VOTED AGAINST MEMBERSHIP (AT THAT TIME OF THE EEC), AND IN 1994 THE BATTLE WAS ON AGAIN. THOSE WHO STOOD BEHIND THIS GREEN DEMONSTRATION IN STORLIDALEN IN SØR-TRØNDELAG GOT THINGS THEIR OWN WAY.

The oil age

Prospecting for oil in the Norwegian sector of the North Sea began in 1966, and the first strike was made on the Christmas weekend of 1969 by the Phillips Petroleum Company. At that time the other oil companies had given up hope, and this was also the last hole Phillips intended to drill. It turned out that the strike was among the biggest in the world, and Norway had become an oil nation!

"The black gold" made it possible to increase state subsidization of agriculture, fisheries, shipping and industry when the international economic crisis hit Norway in 1973. However, although the oil billions contributed to keeping unemployment down, inflation and increasing imports led to Norway's competitive situation worsening. From the end of the 1970s a restrictive economic policy had to be pursued. New laws relating to democracy in the business sector and the working environment increased employees' influence in the work sector, and a special equal opportunities Act was passed. However, the EEC conflict and oil wealth together contributed to creating a right-wing surge in party politics. In the 1970s it was the Conservative Party that increased its support, while the 1990s were characterized by growing support for the neo-liberal Progress Party. However, although the Labour Party lost ground, it was difficult for the centre-right to establish a lasting governmental coalition. Thus, the Labour Party stayed in power in the period from 1973 to 1981 and from 1986 to 1989. After the election in 1989 Jan P. Syse from the Conservative Party formed a centre-right coalition government, but due to disagreement concerning Norway's relationship to the EEC this government had to resign as early as in autumn 1990.

In 1989 the Sami people got their first popularly elected body, Sametinget (the Sami Parliament). This was closely linked to conflicts connected with utilization of the natural resources in Sami areas. The conflict surrounding development of hydro-electric power in the Alta-Kautokeino watercourse was of particular significance. It ended with the river being developed against the will of the Sami people, and this contentious decision forced clarification of the question of rights in the north. The result was the Finnmark Act of 2005, where administration of approximately 95 per cent of the land area in Finnmark was left to a new property company with representatives from the Sami Parliament and the county municipality.

In 1994 the Norwegian people once again said no to membership of the European Union, but at the same time Norway forged strong links with Europe through the EEA agreement. This agreement made Norwegian trade and industry a part of the EU's internal market, with exceptions for agricultural and fisheries products.

In 1990 Gro Harlem Brundtland became Norway's prime minister for the second time, and the Labour Party was in power up to 1997 and again from 2000 to 2001. It was replaced and followed by two minority governments with Kjell Magne Bondevik as prime minister. The Bondevik governments concentrated on tax relief, more competition in the public sector and moderation in public spending. The results of this policy led to a change of government after the election in 2005. Then the Labour Party, Centre Party and the Socialist Left Party formed a "red-green" majority government with Jens Stoltenberg as prime minister.

SINCE THE 1970S THE ENORMOUS CONCRETE STRUCTURES IN THE NORTH SEA HAVE EXTRACTED HUGE DEPOSITS OF OIL AND GAS. THIS HAS GIVEN NORWAY CONSIDERABLE ECONOMIC LEEWAY. THIS SECTOR STANDS FOR MORE THAN 20 PER CENT OF THE COUNTRY'S TOTAL ASSET CREATION, AND A SIGNIFICANT PORTION OF THIS INCOME HAS BEEN INVESTED IN A PETROLEUM FUND THAT IN 2005 CONTAINED MORE THAN 1200 BILLION NORWEGIAN CROWNS.

HRH Crown Prince Haakon and Mette-Marit Tjessem Høiby were married in Oslo Cathedral 25 August 2001. After the wedding the Crown Prince and Crown Princess received the accolade of the people along with the King and Queen, the bridesmaids and the Crown Princess's son, Marius.

World Heritage

The Geiranger Fjord, the pyramids of Egypt, the Victoria Falls in Zambia and Zimbabwe, Machu Picchu in Peru, the Grand Canyon in the USA and the Great Wall of China all have one thing in common: They are among the 812 places found on UNESCO's World Cultural and Natural Heritage List.

UNESCO's Convention on Protection of the World's Cultural and Natural Heritage was ratified in 1972, and was brought about by increasing pressure on natural areas and cultural monuments in the form of wars, conflicts, pollution, natural disasters, the growth of tourism and lack of maintenance. Six years after the Convention was ratified the first twelve places were entered on the list, including the Rock-Hewn Churches and Simen National Park in Ethiopia, L'Anse aux Meadows National Park in Canada, Yellowstone National Park in the USA and the Galápagos Archipelago in the Pacific Ocean.

The Convention has been ratified by 180 countries, and shall contribute to protecting areas or objects that are of such irreplaceable value that they must be regarded as the heritage of the whole of humankind and its coming generations. A special committee evaluates candidates to the list, and strict requirements are placed on follow-up and management of the places listed.

Norway has six places on UNESCO's World Heritage List: Bryggen (the Dock) in Bergen, the Mining Town of Røros, the Rock Drawings of Alta, Urnes Stave Church, the Vega Archipelago and the West Norwegian Fjord Landscape.

Urnes Stave Church

As early as around 1030 travellers on the Luster Fjord in Sogn og Fjordane could look up at the church building at Ornes, "the nose that protrudes from the mountain". The fact is that hidden beneath Urnes Stave Church there are traces of two smaller churches, the first of which was probably built early in the 11th century, during the transition from the belief in Norse gods to Christianity. From written sources too we know that the new religion soon took a good grip on the people of Sogn; Snorre Sturlason (1179-1241) writes that Olav Tryggvason Christianized the district by force in 997. Both the church's interior and the liturgy must have made a powerful impression on the congregation of the time, standing there surrounded by the most beautiful ecclesiastical art illuminated by flickering candle-light, enveloped by the scent of incense, the sound of choral song and mass bells and the unfamiliar Latin chanting of the priest.

The structural supports of a stave church consist of vertical posts called staves, from which the name is derived. These are bound together, two by two, with sills above and below, so that they form a framework that the wall-planks can be inserted into. The stave churches represent our finest handicraft tradition within construction, material selection and décor, and are an extremely valuable part of the Norwegian cultural heritage. They are the country's oldest preserved wooden buildings and Norway's most important contribution to world architecture. Originally there were more than 1000 stave churches in Norway, but many were pulled down after a law was passed in 1851 stating that the church in each parish should have room for at least three tenths of the population. Only 28 stave churches have been preserved today.

Urnes Stave Church was finished around 1150, and is the oldest of our preserved stave churches, which is partly due to the fact that the timber rests on a stone foundation that separates the old logs from damp earth and prevents gradual rotting. Urnes Stave Church would not have seen great changes before the Reformation in 1537, but with the Lutheran ban on worshipping saints, much of the oldest ecclesiastical art disappeared. Gradually churches got benches, a pulpit and an altar piece – and as more people learned to read, the need emerged for better lighting in the interior of the church, leading to windows.

The original churches at Ornes must have been extraordinarily beautiful and exquisitely formed. We can see that from the building components that were re-used on Urnes Stave Church, such as the portal in the northern wall, the carved wall-planks and the richly decorated corner post in the chancel. The motif represents a struggle between what probably were lions and snakes, and the carvings have been dated to around 1050. This is the art of wood-carving at a very high level, and the originators' choice of motif and craftsmanship has subsequently given name and content to the Urnes style. Urnes Stave Church was included in UNESCO's World Cultural and Natural Heritage List in 1979.

The West Norwegian Fjord Landscape

THE FIRST HUMAN BEINGS to make their homes in the rugged mountain landscape along the fjords of West Norway, came shortly after the ice receded 10,000 years ago. Since there was easy access by sea to the fjords, they were used for transport purposes long before the Viking period – they carried people, animals and goods between the mainland and the coast, both in summer and in winter, as the warm Gulf Stream provides this area with a mild climate with ice-free winters. However, the fjords have also separated people and settlements from one another, thus contributing to considerable variations in dialect.

In 2005 the Geiranger Fjord in Møre og Romsdal and the Nærøy Fjord in Sogn og Fjordane were included in UNESCO's World Cultural and Natural Heritage List under the name "West Norwegian Fjord Landscape". These spectacular representatives of the classic fjord landscape are unique in a global perspective. The Geiranger Fjord and Nærøy Fjord are situated on either side of Europe's largest glacier, the Jostedal Glacier, which covers an area as great as 487 square kilometres. And it was precisely these enormous masses of ice which had previously covered most of Northern Europe, that carved out the Norwegian fjords by gouging away half-a-millimeter of bedrock a year over a period of 2.5 million years.

The Nærøy Fjord is the wildest and most beautiful of the lateral arms of the Sogne Fjord, and moreover the narrowest fjord in the world. A boat-trip on the 17-kilometre long fjord is one of the most dramatic natural experiences Europe can offer. The snow-covered mountains rise up to 1800 metres above the glittering surface of the sea, while the fjord is only 250 metres wide at its narrowest point.

The Geiranger Fjord, which is situated 120 kilometres farther north, is also part of a larger fjord system where it turns off from a lateral arm of Storfjorden. It is reckoned to be among the very finest fjord landscapes in the world. Innumerable waterfalls, such as "The Bride's Veil" and "The Seven Sisters" tumble down from the sheer cliff faces, while numerous rivers run from glaciers and jagged mountains straight down into the fjord. It is understandable that UNESCO is of the opinion that not just the fjords themselves but also the surrounding landscape deserves to be preserved. High above the water, upon fertile mountain shelves, lie farms and summer dairies – with people still living in some of them.

UNESCO is far from being alone in appreciating the Norwegian fjords. They are among Norway's most visited natural attractions, and the first tourist ship entered the Geiranger Fjord as early as in 1869. But although the Geiranger Fjord and Nærøy Fjord have been tourist destinations for over 150 years, they were crowned "the world's top unspoiled travel destination" by *National Geographic Traveler Magazine* in 2004.

Bryggen (The Dock) in Bergen

BERGEN WAS FOUNDED by King Olav Kyrre around 1070. As early as the 13th century the city was an administrative focal point for church and kingdom and an important centre of international trade. The population of Norway had grown considerably, and the country lacked grain for consumption. The German Baltic towns had this, and in the 14th century the king had to grant special rights to merchants from Bremen and Lübeck and other members of the Hanseatic Union. The Hanseatics established one of their most important trading offices in Bergen around 1360, and came to dominate this important transhipment port for grain and dried fish for almost 400 years.

At Bryggen a community of German merchants and craftsmen grew forth. On the east side of Vågen, in front of Bryggen's characteristic rows of buildings, lay ships from most European ports. These carried grain, wine, textiles and pottery to Norway, and took away dried fish. This was in great demand, particularly during fasting periods in Catholic countries. When the dried fish arrived in Bergen from North Norway, the quay and booths hummed with life.

Not until the 20th century did the original use of the Bryggen area cease. The emergence of the industrial age led to new demands for efficient storage and transportation of goods, and the old harbour quarter soon became

unsuitable. The traditional trade in dried fish gradually died out and a 700–800-year-old tradition was broken.

The southern part of Bryggen was demolished early in the 20th century, while the northern part was declared a protected area in 1927. In connection with a major conflagration in 1955 half of the part that remained standing was reduced to ashes, and now only a fourth of the original buildings are left. The remaining 58 buildings have been given protected status. The remains of several hundred buildings have been excavated since extensive archaeological surveys were implemented after the great fire of 1955.

The tenement buildings at Bryggen consisted of one or two long rows, so-called double tenements, divided into several rooms, with a common passageway. They were combined homes and store-rooms, two or three storeys high. A stroll through Bryggen's narrow passageways is like taking a trip into the semi-darkness of history. However, Bryggen in Bergen is not a museum; on the contrary it is a district full of life, with handicraft businesses, restaurants, shops and offices. The characteristic parallel rows of buildings with gables facing the sea are a type of architecture that has existed for almost 900 years. Bryggen in Bergen was included in UNESCO's World Cultural and Natural Heritage List in 1979.

The Mining Town of Røros

SEVERAL HUNDRED YEARS of mining operations and "urban agriculture" have created a distinctive urban environment in the midst of a Norwegian mountain plateau. However, with its 5600 inhabitants Røros does not have city status – it is a mining town, a designation it shares only with Kongsberg, which was known for its silver mines.

The rich deposits of copper at Røros were discovered by chance by a farmer, Hans Aasen, when he was hunting reindeer at Storvola. This was the starting-signal for the establishment of Røros Copperworks in 1644, and of what in time was to become the mining town of Røros, a community based on copper-mining and the smelting of copper ore. The first and largest smelting works  was built at the waterfall in the Hitter River where Røros is situated today, while the mines are located up in the mountains around the mining town. Røros Copperworks closed down in 1977, after 333 years of operation. The author Johan Falkberget (1879–1967) began his working career as a miner in Røros, and he used this environment as the background to most of his literary production. Besides the Røros Museum, his home, Ratvolden, is the most well-known and often visited museum in Røros.

In addition to mining, agriculture was a part of the basis for Røros's existence, and these two commercial activities created a form of symbiosis. In times of recession, or if the mines were not being worked, the inhabitants could live from their livestock, and since they owned the land and property themselves, they were tied to the place and remained living there in bad times too. In this way Røros Copperworks ensured that it had a stable workforce – moreover the farms produced oxen and horses for the extensive transport activity linked to mining operations.

With its old wooden buildings Røros represents a living cultural heritage, which is based on acombination of continental ideas and ancient Norwegian building customs. Here the farm, with its buildings for people and livestock gathered around a square yard, has been moved from the countryside into the town. The streets form a network characteristic of the Renaissance towns, but when Røros was torched by Swedish soldiers in 1678 and 1679, Baroque was the current style in vogue in Europe. Thus, when the mining town was rebuilt after the fires, the main street, Storgata, was broadened at the lower end, while it gradually narrowed upwards. This measure, the "false perspective" of the Baroque period, provides the street with an impressive feeling of depth.

With its 1600 seats, Røros Church, "Bcrgstadcns Ziir", is the third largest in Norway, and since 1784 it has towered over the low, densely-packed, wooden buildings like a singular landmark of stone. However, it was the unique wooden buildings from the 18th and 19th centuries that led Røros on to UNESCO's World Cultural and Natural Heritage List.

The Vega Archipelago

THE VEGA ARCHIPELAGO shows how generations of fishermen/farmers have maintained a sustainable living rich in tradition along an extremely weather-beaten coast just south of the Arctic Circle. The now unique harvesting of the eider duck down has been a crucial commercial practice throughout the past 1500 years, largely carried out by women. While the men were out fishing, it was the women who gathered eggs and down. The best down stations were situated farthest out to sea, and about a hundred years ago the biggest farms had a good 1000 brooding eider ducks each. For many centuries the eider duck was the most common farm animal on this archipelago.

Today the Vega Archipelago covers an area of 1037 square kilometres and consists of over 6500 islands, islets and skerries off the coast of Helgeland in North Norway. The archipelago illustrates the great importance of the Gulf Stream to the settlements along the coast of our part of the world. The oldest traces of human beings on Vega have been dated to the Stone Age, 10,000 years in the past. This is the earliest confirmed settlement in North Norway, and there is reason to believe that the plentiful fish resources around the island contributed to people choosing to remain living there.

However, eggs and down have also played an important role for the coastal populace, both as food and a source of income, and the availability of these resources has contributed to forming the pattern of settlement in many places in North Norway. From sources such as the historian Snorre Sturlason (1179–1241) we know that down and eggs from this area were a well-known commercial product as early as in Viking times, and Archbishop Olaus Magnus refers to egg and down stations in his history of the Nordic peoples from 1555. At this time demand increased considerably, and in order to safeguard the down and eggs for themselves, local station owners began to declare egg and down stations protected areas.

The cultural landscape of the Vega Archipelago consists of islets for grazing and haymaking, various beacons and a collection of buildings that bear unique witness to people's life and work. On a majority of the islands there are sea farms with boathouses, outhouses and living quarters for both people and eider ducks. Since the 1950s most of the islands have become depopulated, but in the summer season the former islanders still go out to look after their farm animals, the eider ducks.

The Vega Archipelago was included in UNESCO's World Cultural and Natural Heritage List in 2004, and we can merely hope that this will contribute to protecting the archipelago's distinctive cultural landscape and the unique and rich tradition of eider duck farming.

The Rock Drawings of Alta

THE ROCK DRAWINGS of Alta are the largest known collection of petroglyphs created by hunting people. The first rock drawings were discovered in this area in 1972, and as the 1970s progressed a number of new discoveries were made. Today the number of figures is estimated to be more than 5000, and more are continually being found. They are distributed across five areas, one containing rock paintings and four containing rock engravings. A number of the rock paintings were already known when the rock engravings were found. The biggest area is situated at Alta museum in Hjemmeluft/Jiepmaolukta, with at least 3000 figures. Some of the areas around the museum have been made available to the public, and about 70,000 people visit Alta Museum each year. The Rock Drawings of Alta were included in UNESCO's World Cultural and Natural Heritage List in 1985, and are the only prehistoric cultural monument in Norway included in this list.

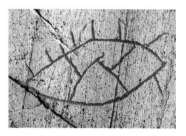

Petroglyphs is a common international designation that includes engravings as well as paintings and drawings. On UNESCO's list you will find examples of petroglyphs from every continent, among others Kakadu National Park in Australia, Sierra da Capivara National Park in Brazil, the Rock Drawings of Dazu in China, the Ajantu Caves in India, the rock drawing areas of Tadart Acasus in Libya, and not least the famous Altamira Cave in Spain.

Petroglyphs cannot be dated directly using current methods, but must be interpreted in relation to motif, design and location in the landscape, and be seen in the context of other archaeological finds. The pictures in Alta were created by hunters and catchers between 6200 and 2000 years ago, and give us a glimpse of their daily life, religious conceptions and rituals. Many of the figures are of high artistic quality and are very well preserved. Here we find reproductions of human beings, boats, tools, and various geometric patterns and figures. Often you will see extensive scenes where people and animals participate in various activities, such as hunting, catching and fishing, dancing and rituals. The animals depicted, among others reindeer, moose, bears, hares, geese, halibut, salmon and whales, also provide us with an insight into the natural surroundings and basic resources of humans. A particular feature of the Rock Drawings of Alta is that the place was evidently used as a venue for ritual practices over such a long period of time. For 4200 years people have been coming back here and creating new Rock Drawings. A number of researchers think that this may have been an important meeting-place for people from the coastal and inland areas. They would have met one another here, perhaps in connection with seasonal relocation, and performed various rituals.

WESTERN NORWAY

THIS REGION CONSISTS OF four counties, from Rogaland in the south to Møre og Romsdal in the north, all of them with the sea as their neighbour in the west. The Sogne Fjord, the world's longest fjord, divides West Norway in two, stretching 204 kilometres into the country from the North Sea towards Jotunheimen National Park with its majestic mountain peaks. North of the Sogne Fjord lies Europe's largest glacier, the Jostedal Glacier, covering an area of all of 487 square kilometres. This region also boasts Europe's biggest mountain plateau, the Hardanger Plateau. And it is precisely these spectacular fjords, waterfalls, mountains and glaciers that most people associate with this part of Norway.

Perhaps West Norway is best known for having the most beautiful fjord landscapes in the world (see page 38). Along the Geiranger Fjord you can see innumerable waterfalls tumbling from the sheer cliff faces straight down into the fjord. Farther south lies the Hardanger Fjord, surrounded by flowering orchards, and the Lyse Fjord where the towering Preacher's Pulpit provides an unforgettable view for those who dare to approach its jutting edge. Alongside the fjords small, meagre farms cling tenaciously to the mountain shelves, but here you will also find magnificent estates and timber hotels in dragon style, erected during the childhood of tourism in the 19th century.

With its enormous areas of unspoiled nature the region provides opportunities for varied leisure activities all year round, whether it be mountain-climbing, skiing and walking trips, glacier tours, cycling or fishing. You can travel by boat along the coast and into one of the beautiful fjords. Touring motorists can experience the unique coastal stretch of the Atlantic Ocean Highway which launches itself from skerry to skerry at the very outermost points of the coast, or Trollstigen's winding ascent alongside sheer drops a little farther inland.

At Jæren, in the very south, however, it is not high, sheer-faced mountains that characterize the landscape. Here you will find long beaches, low, white houses and flat fields divided by roads and stone fences. Farther north in the same county lies the petroleum capital city of Stavanger (see page 74), which contains one of Europe's oldest intact collections of wooden buildings, a picturesque district from the age of the sailing ships, with white-painted houses bordering narrow alleyways. The old Hanseatic city of Bergen (see page 76) is the birthplace of the composer Edvard Grieg as well as the gateway to the fjord region and point of departure for the Coastal Express. The western Norwegian coastal towns of Haugesund, Ålesund, Molde and Kristiansund were founded thanks to the rich resources of the sea, but western Norwegian coastal culture is also visible as small, old trading stations along the coast. They have lost much of their function from the time the boat was the most important means of transport, but many of them are becoming very popular tourist destinations.

Fruit trees blooming in Hardanger, one of Norway's most beautiful natural areas, are a wonderful attraction. This is from Ullensvang overlooking Sørfjorden, a lateral arm of the Hardanger Fjord. Hordaland.

Fresh ski-trails run from the small red cabin at Vikafjellet in Sogn og Fjordane.
The boat leaning against the cabin wall will certainly not be used for a few months …

The old road from Storfjorden leading into Viddalssetra where we find the Kalveskrednipa peak in the background (1488 m above sea-level). Møre og Romsdal.

The evening sun hanging low over the Sunnmørsalpene mountains is reflected in the Brekketindene peaks. Farther behind lies the famous Slogen peak (1564 m above sea-level), and at the very back we can just see Jakta. Møre og Romsdal.

THE FAMED RAUMA SALMON RIVER ORIGINATES IN THE LESJASKOGSVATNET LAKE, AND ON ITS WAY TO THE SEA IT VARIES IN INTENSITY BETWEEN LANGUID STRETCHES AND BOILING WHITEWATER. THERE CAN HARDLY BE A RIVER THAT FLOWS THROUGH A MORE BEAUTIFUL NATURAL LANDSCAPE. BEFORE POURING INTO THE SEA THE RAUMA ALSO PASSES BY THE RENOWNED TROLLVEGGEN. MØRE OG ROMSDAL.

THE PRIEST'S PULPIT IS ONE OF NORWAY'S MOST SPECTACULAR ATTRACTIONS WITH ITS 604-METRE VERTICAL DROP DOWN INTO LYSEFJORDEN EAST OF STAVANGER, ROGALAND.

Many long-since vacated fjord and mountain farms lie along the Geiranger Fjord. From Blomberg (452 m above sea-level) you have a view of the "Seven Sisters" waterfalls and "The Suitor". Møre og Romsdal.

A NAVIGATION MARKER ON A LITTLE REEF IS MIRRORED IN KJØSNESFJORDEN. SOGN OG FJORDANE.

THE PILOT'S BOAT HAS JUST PASSED THROUGH SØRE VAULEN, THE SEA-LANE BETWEEN BERGSØY AND NERLANDSØYA IN SUNNMØRE. MØRE OG ROMSDAL.

High above Synnulvsfjorden in Sunnmøre lies the old farm of Meåkneset. Here the houses were built together in a row below the moun-tainside to protect people and livestock from the huge avalanches that threatened to roar down in winter. Møre og Romsdal.

THE RUNDE LIGHTHOUSE IS SITUATED ON KVALNESET, ON THE NORTHWEST EDGE OF THE RUNDE BIRD SANCTUARY IN HERØY KOMMUNE, MØRE OG ROMSDAL.
THE LIGHTHOUSE WAS INAUGURATED IN 1767, AS THE FIFTH LIGHTHOUSE IN NORWAY AFTER LINDESNES.

The spectacular Atlantic Ocean Road consists among other things of eight bridges between islets in a beautiful natural area on the coast of Nordmøre. This unique road and bridge project, which spans eight kilometres, was opened in 1989, and has been crowned the structure of the century in Norway. Møre og Romsdal.

Over thousands of years the sea has formed the Kannesteinen rock formation which is situated on the shoreline at Oppedal in Sogn og Fjordane.

Through Sunndalen in Møre og Romsdal runs the well-known Driva salmon river, which originates in Dovre.

THE EVENING SUN BATHES THE MOUNTAINS ABOVE GEIRANGER IN COLOUR, BUT THE REDDISH HUE DOES NOT REACH DOWN TO THE TINY CABIN IN BREIDALEN.
MØRE OG ROMSDAL.

The autumn hues on the trees create a beautiful contrast to the new-fallen snow in the mountains. Ulstein, Møre og Romsdal.

In front of the mighty Folgefonna glacier lies the Borsheimsholmen skerry framed by Hissfjorden, a lateral arm of the 180-kilometer long Hardanger Fjord. Kvam, Hordaland.

On the mountain pass between Åheim and Maurstad lies the Bekslevatnet lake, which abounds in mountain trout. Møre og Romsdal.

Rundebrua, situated outside Ålesund in Møre og Romsdal, takes you over to the largest of the big Norwegian island bird sanctuaries. The cliff bird sanctuary of *Rundebranden* is host to a unique multiplicity of species.

Opposite page: A puffin in silhouette at Runde in Herøy. The evening light hides its characteristic red, yellow and blue-coloured beak

STAVANGER

STAVANGER IS BEAUTIFULLY situated between the two fjords Gandsfjord and Hafrsfjord, the latter being the place that has symbolized the unification of Norway since Harald Hårfagre and his men won a decisive battle here in 880 AD. The first human beings to arrive came to this area more than 10,000 years ago, and one of the oldest settlements in Norway was recently excavated just south of the city.

Norway's petroleum capital was granted city status as early as in 1125, when Stavanger became a bishopric and construction of the beautiful Cathedral was started. The city grew slowly in the area around the church, but as a centre of trade Stavanger remained in the shadow of Bergen to the north throughout the Middle Ages. The development from a small town to a relatively big city by Norwegian standards did not begin before the early 19th century, when herring fisheries experienced a sensational growth. Throughout history the economic and employment situation in the Stavanger region has been based on handicrafts, agriculture, fishing, shipping, boatbuilding and the canning industry, but since 1970 Stavanger has been the main base for petroleum activities in the North Sea. The city is also an important communications centre. It has an airport at Sola, is the terminus of the South Norway railway, is bypassed by the E 39 highway along the coast between Kristiansand and Trondheim and has a number of important ferry routes.

FOUNDED: 1125
POPULATION: 114,000
AREA: 70 KM2
COUNTY: ROGALAND

By boat you can visit the beautiful Kvitsøy Archipelago off the coast, or travel into the Lyse Fjord, where you will find the characteristic Preacher's Pulpit overlooking the fjord. The Utstein Monastery outside Stavanger is Norway's best preserved monastery, and in the medieval church concerts are often held, partly in collaboration with the International Chamber Music Festival in Stavanger.

Stavanger is an exciting combination of old and new. The city's petroleum museum is one of Norway's foremost examples of modern architecture, but northern Europe's best preserved wooden buildings are also situated here in an idyllic district with small, white wooden houses from the time of the sailing ships. Stavanger has a number of fine museums and cultural institutions, and has been designated as European Cultural Capital in 2008.

BERGEN

FROM THE TOP OF FLØYEN (302 m. above sea-level), one of the seven mountains that ring Bergen, you can look down on Vågen where King Olav Kyrre sailed in and founded the city in the year 1070. As early as the 13th century Bergen had become an important centre of international trade, and up to 1299 it was Norway's capital city. For a period in the Middle Ages it was the largest city in Scandinavia, not least because the Hanseatics established one of their most important trading offices here around 1360. Bryggen in Bergen (see page 40) is a well-preserved memorial of the time when Bergen was a trading and seafaring city of European significance. Trade and shipping have always been of great importance to the city and are still an important part of business life in Bergen. Industry, handicrafts, tourism, fisheries and petroleum and gas activities are other important business sectors.

However this centre of commerce has also evolved into one of Norway's most important cultural arenas. The birthplace of Edvard Grieg has one of the world's oldest symphony orchestras, international festivals are arranged here, and the city's theatre – where Henrik Ibsen was instructor in the 1850s – is the oldest in Norway. Visitors can also choose among many fine museums, including a quite unique collection of Edvard Munch's pictures.

FOUNDED: 1070
POPULATION: 240,000
AREA: 465 KM²
COUNTY: HORDALAND

But it is more than its cultural life that makes Bergen a popular destination for Norwegian and foreign tourists. The city is the gateway to the Norwegian fjords, situated as it is between the Sogne Fjord and the Hardanger Fjord, and it has one of Europe's biggest harbours for visiting cruise-ships. Bergen is also the point of departure for the Coastal Express and the terminus of the Bergen Railway, and it has an international airport just a few kilometres from the city centre.

When the incomparable Fløibanen Funicular has brought travellers safely back down from Fløyen and the magnificent view of the fjord, mountains and city, they can visit the Fishmarket and Bryggen, stroll between charming wooden houses in the narrow alleyways of the Old Town or visit Edvard Griegs home at Troldhaugen.

SOUTHERN NORWAY

The coast of South Norway became ice-free about 11,000 years ago, and shortly afterwards the first hunters and catchers settled in a district with survival conditions not unlike those we presently find on Svalbard and the west coast of Greenland. Here there were plenty of fish, shellfish and pollack, and on the moors you could hunt reindeer, moose, hart and bear. The rock drawings from the Bronze Age found on the Lista Peninsula show stylized ships and small, round pits that symbolize the sun. By worshipping the sun and the ship, the Bronze Age people wanted to ensure good fortune for agriculture, forestry and shipping, business sectors that have been important to this region's inhabitants all the way up to modern times.

Southern Norwegians and new arrivals have continued to cultivate the sun and the ship, although for quite different reasons than in the Bronze Age. This coast is the closest we get to a Riviera in Norway, with a magnificent skerry coastline, white wooden houses, summer cottages and small motorized sailboats chugging by. Throughout a long, cold winter many Norwegians dream of eating prawns on one of the many skerries or islets, diving from sea-smoothed rocks, drying themselves in the sun and rambling through the streets licking a large ice-cream.

. Small southern towns lie along the coast like pearls on a string, with white houses between flowering gardens and newly-painted picket fences. Among the most beautiful ones are Lillesand, Tvedestrand, Risør, Brekkestø, Gamle Hellesund and Ny-Hellesund. Lyngør, which is situated far out on the coast, and has wooden houses closely grouped around its cozy harbour, was designated Europe's best preserved urbanization a few years ago. South Norway's capital city, Kristiansand (see page 92), is a charming city with old, weather-beaten houses and a pulsating life in summertime. The best known attraction is the city's theme park, Dyreparken – the Zoo.

Farther inland the terrain and vegetation are more varied, eminently suitable for those who wish to hunt, fish, or go mountain-climbing or rafting in one of the rivers. Setesdal, with its beautiful moors, numerous fishing lakes and large pasturelands, has preserved the traditions of the countryside and the old farming culture well. The valley is renowned for its beautiful folk music, its well-preserved old houses and its handicraft traditions.

Until a hundred years ago Norway's southernmost region was regarded as a part of West Norway, something that the poet Vilhelm Krag – among many others – found extremely inappropriate. Why couldn't the area have its own identity and designation? The so-called *soft coastal strip* and the region of South Norway were 'invented' by Krag on Sunday 16 March 1902, when the *Morgenbladet* newspaper printed an article entitled 'Norwegians'. There the brand-new term South Norway was launched, giving pleasure to the many who pronounced Norwegian words with soft consonants.

Ever since the Middle Ages Lindesnes in Vest-Agder has been an important landsighting between the North Sea and the Baltic. Many a ship has gone down in these treacherous waters, and it was no accident that Norway's first lighthouse was lit precisely here in 1655, on the command of King Fredrik III. It was a three-storey tower, built of wood, with 30 wax candles that fluttered behind a leaded window. The first lighthouse was short-lived, and in 1725 a more modern coal-fired lighthouse came into permanent operation.

KNABEN, TO THE FAR NORTH OF KVINESDAL BORDERING ON THE HIGH MOUNTAIN PLATEAU, IS A POPULAR OPEN-AIR VENUE WITH WELL-MARKED TRAILS LEADING INTO THE HILLS. VEST-AGDER.

Old Hellesund, with its characteristic white southern Norwegian houses, is beautifully situated along the Blindleia inner shipping lane between Lillesand and Kristiansand. Aust-Agder.

The Ny-Hellesund archipelago is a summer paradise in the Søgne skerry landscape of Vest-Agder. Now peace and tranquillity reign over the old trading post which was a centre of shipping traffic along the coast for several hundred years.

OUTSIDE BREKKESTO LIE THE SKERRIES AND REEFS THAT PROVIDE PROTECTION AGAINST THE HIGH SEAS LIKE A STRING OF PEARLS ENCIRCLING THIS IDYLLIC SOUTHERN NORWEGIAN TOWNSHIP. LILLESAND, AUST-AGDER.

Dusk has settled upon the tiny township of Snig, on the way towards Lindesnes Lighthouse. Vest-Agder.

IN THE ERA OF THE SAILING SHIPS IN THE 1850S MORE THAN 800 PEOPLE RESIDED AND EARNED A LIVING ON LYNGØR. TODAY THE ARCHIPELAGO HAS 120 PERMANENT INHABITANTS.

OPPOSITE PAGE: IN 1990 THE ISLAND COMMUNITY OF LYNGØR IN TVEDESTRAND MUNICIPALITY, AUST-AGDER, WAS CROWNED EUROPE'S BEST PRESERVED URBANIZATION. IT IS EXTREMELY POPULAR AS A HOLIDAY RESORT AND HARBOUR FOR BOATING TOURISTS IN SUMMER.

KRISTIANSAND

THE CAPITAL CITY of South Norway is named after its founder, King Christian IV. He granted the place city privileges in 1641 and had it built with the typical right-angled streets which still characterize the city centre. Before Kristiansand was founded there was no city between Skien and Stavanger. With its strategic location as a trading centre and its fine harbour, Kristiansand was very important, particularly during the great wars in Europe, when access to the Baltic Sea was partly blocked to shipping. In 1682 the king decided that the bishopric should be moved from Stavanger to Kristiansand, which proved important to the growth and identity of the city. However, Christian IV's plans for the city were ambitious – they assumed a population of 20,000 – and it took close to 300 years before the city approached this number of inhabitants. Today Kristiansand is an important transport and communication link, and in addition it has become the region's centre of trade, industry and higher education.

FOUNDED: 1641
POPULATION: 77,000
AREA: 276 KM²
COUNTY: VEST-AGDER

The term 'Idyllic South Norway' is associated by most Norwegians with sun-warmed skerries, crystal-clear water, inviting beaches and small, white houses in lush gardens by the sea. This description fits Kristiansand and the surrounding area well, which in the summer season sees its population multiplied by the tourists who stream in from home and abroad. This strip of coast, with its beautiful islets protecting the country from the pounding seas of the Skagerrak, experiences the most days of sunshine in Norway. From Kristiansand it's only a short way to the idyllic skerries, and a few kilometres from the coast lies the paradise for all Norwegian children, Kristiansand Zoo and Amusement Park, with monkeys, tigers and pirate ships with 'real' pirates. Those who have grown out of the Zoo's attractions prefer to visit Norway's greatest festival of music, *the Quart Festival*, which is held at the beginning of July each year. It was in this city that the Crown Princess of Norway, Mette-Marit Tjessem Høiby, met HRH Crown Prince Haakon for the first time.

EASTERN NORWAY

THIS REGION INCLUDES BOTH coastal and inland counties, and altogether more than half of the inhabitants of Norway live in the eight counties that comprise this region. East Norway can provide you with a varied landscape that stretches from undulating, flat agricultural areas to dramatic mountain massifs.

Farthest inside the Oslo Fjord lies the capital city with its beautiful natural surroundings. Most of Norway's governmental bodies are situated in Oslo (see page 114), but the city is also the centre of business and culture, and visitors can choose from a wide variety of attractions. Norway's main airport, Gardermoen, is situated to the north of Oslo, in the densely populated county of Akershus.

To the south, along the Oslo Fjord, you will find many idyllic islands, small communities and towns, including Norway's oldest town, Tønsberg, founded in 871. In the Middle Ages this town had the country's largest citadel with a royal palace and Franciscan monastery. The county of Vestfold has been known for its links with shipping ever since the time of the sagas, and it was here that most of the best known Viking ships were excavated. On the other side of the fjord lies Fredrikstad with its fortress from the 17th century and a charming old town situated on the east side of Norway's longest river, Glomma. The county of Østfold has the greatest concentration of monuments of the past, including a number of areas containing petroglyphs.

To the west of the Oslo Fjord we find the counties of Buskerud and Telemark, which both contain a part of Europe's highest mountain plateau, the Hardanger Plateau. Here beautiful, convoluted valleys such as Numedal and Hallingdal wind their way through the landscape and built-up areas that are rich in tradition and folk art. The extensive hydro-electric resources gave this region a central role during the country's industrialization. The old silver-mining town of Kongsberg has a number of fine museums, and in Telemark we find the mountain village of Morgedal, which is said to be the cradle of the sport of skiing.

North of Oslo we find Mjøsa, Norway's largest lake (362 square kilometres), ringed by some of the most fertile areas of the country. Hamar is the port of call of the world's oldest paddle steamer, "Skibladner". The ruins of one of the country's most beautiful churches are to be found encapsulated in a magnificent protective cocoon of glass. In summer you can travel on from here with "Skibladner" to Lillehammer, the town that arranged the Winter Olympic Games in 1994. Farther north in the winter sports county of Oppland, the long Gudbrandsdalen valley lies between towering, unspoiled mountainous areas such as Rondane, Dovre and Jotunheimen. Valdres is the other great valley in Oppland, and it is also rich in ancient building culture and folk art. Three Norwegians have received the Nobel Prize in literature; Bjørnstjerne Bjørnson, Knut Hamsun and Sigrid Undset. They all had close links to this county, and in May every year a great festival of literature is held in Lillehammer, where Sigrid Undset lived.

THE SETTING SUN HAS CAST A BEAUTIFUL VEIL OVER SØMÅKVOLVET IN ENGERDAL, HEDMARK. MANY POPULAR SMALL FISHING LAKES ARE LOCATED HERE, AND BOTH IN SUMMER AND WINTER PATIENT SOULS CAN CATCH TROUT, CHAR OR GRAYLING

A YELLOWING CORNFIELD IN AUGUST AT HAMMERSTAD FARM IN STANGE, ONE OF THE FERTILE LOWLAND FARMING COMMUNITIES AT MJØSA, HEDMARK.

The Moon rises above the Jotunheimen National Park, viewed from Bjørnungen (2110 m above sea-level) towards the southeast. Oppland.

A quiet forest pool at Flenkjølen in Rendalen, which is Southern Norway's largest inland municipality, with unusually rich opportunities for hunting, fishing and outdoor pursuits. Hedmark.

The snowstorm erases the colours in the ancient cultural landscape, but both the birch and the stone wall have been exposed to hard weather before. Oppland.

The Northern Lights (*AURORA BOREALIS*) are mirrored in the Vesle Rokosjøen Wild Life Preserve. Løten, Hedmark.

GLÁMA IDLES QUIETLY BY HÅMMÅLSFJELLET (1543 M ABOVE SEA-LEVEL) IN THE MOUNTAIN MUNICIPALITY OF OS, TO THE FAR NORTH OF HEDMARK.

In the far south of the island of Tjøme in Vestfold lies the open-air venue of Verdens Ende (the World's End) with its innumerable islets and skerries. The magnificent view of the Skagerrak suggests that before the 20TH century the area was frequently used as a vantage point for pilots looking for jobs.

From Trysilfjellet a brook flows placidly between heather, marsh flowers and evergreens. Trysil, Hedmark.

Behind this burial mound from the Bronze Age the waves of the Skagerrak splash against the pebble beach at Mølen. In this unique ancient landscape lie 230 manmade cairns, which may have been the burial ground of a branch of the powerful Ynglinge dynasty. The most recent cairns stem from the Viking period, but the oldest burial mounds may stem from before the birth of Christ. Larvik, Vestfold.

THE DYING RAYS OF THE SUN FILTER THROUGH SNOW-LADEN SPRUCE TREES AT SJUSJØEN. RINGSAKER, HEDMARK.

OPPOSITE PAGE: WIND AND SNOW HAVE PACKED IN A CAIRN ON STORE RAMSHØGDA (1463 M ABOVE SEA-LEVEL) ON THE OUTSKIRTS OF RONDANE NATIONAL PARK. SØR-FRON, OPPLAND.

Oslo

THE CITY'S UNIQUE LOCATION between fjord and forestland, with excellent communications both by land and sea, was undoubtedly a good reason why settlements appeared here in their time. The city was founded by King Harald Hardråde around the year 1050, when he had a palace built in the present Old Town, but the first signs of urban development go all the way back to the year 900. When King Håkon V initiated work on Akershus Palace and Fortress around the year 1300, Oslo was already an important trading town. During the period of union with Denmark, however, the city lost its status as capital and stagnated economically. In 1624 the city was completely destroyed by fire, and King Christian IV decided that it should be moved to the area around Akershus Fortress and be renamed Christiania. In this area, which is called the Quadrature, today we find a number of streets and buildings from the 17th century.

Christiania again became the capital in 1814, when Norway got its own constitution, and the 19th century was a period of considerable expansion. A number of public buildings, such as the Royal Palace, the Storting (the Norwegian Parliament), the University and the National Theatre were erected at this time, and they can all be viewed along Oslo's main promenade, Karl Johan's Street. After the dissolution of the union with Sweden in 1905, nationalistic feelings were strong – many people disliked the fact that the capital city was named after a Danish king, and in 1925 the city took back the name of Oslo.

Most of Norway's governmental bodies are situated in Oslo, but in addition to its functions as a capital city it is also the centre of commerce and culture. The city contains many important cultural institutions and tourist attractions, and even tourists on short day-trips find time to see the Munch Museum, the Vigeland Park, the Holmenkollen Ski-Jump, the Viking Ship Museum and take a stroll through the new district of Aker Brygge, a dockside area with trendy restaurants and other facilities facing Akershus Fortress. Those with more time available can choose among a rich and varied selection of cultural attractions and entertainment facilities, both in daytime and at night.

Oslo's location, and the fact that only 1/3 of its area has seen urban development, makes the city an eldorado for open-air enthusiasts. Both the wooded hinterland and the fjord, with its small idyllic islands, are constantly visited and used by the city's inhabitants, both in summertime and in wintertime.

FOUNDED: 1050
POPULATION: 535,000
AREA: 454 KM²
COUNTY: OSLO

CENTRAL NORWAY

IN MANY WAYS THE VARIED NATURE of Trøndelag's counties is like a microcosm of Norway. Behind broad agricultural settlements lie huge mountains and great plateaus. Forests cover large parts of the region, and stretch out all the way to the rugged coast, which is protected by a multitude of large and small islands. Two of the largest ones are Frøya and Hitra, which have subsea connections with the mainland. Beyond these islands starts the Trondheim Fjord, stretching 126 kilometres inland, to Steinkjer, the administrative centre of Nord-Trøndelag. In this county lies the well-known salmon river, Namsen, but also farther south in Trøndelag you will find a number of rivers bulging with salmon and trout.

In Sør-Trøndelag lies the extremely well-preserved Mining Town of Røros (see page 42), Norway's only mountain town. This town, with its unique church and many characteristic wooden buildings is on UNESCO's list of cultural monuments worthy of conservation. Today it is modern industry, trade and tourism that characterize the mining town, along with the primary industries of agriculture and reindeer-tending in the surrounding area.

This region plays a crucial role in the history of Norway; it has been said that if you took everything related to Trøndelag out of the history books, only the covers would be left. Among the many historical places are Stiklestad in Nord-Trøndelag, where the canonized king, Olav Haraldsson, fell in battle 29 July 1030. Here they perform the 'Play on Saint Olav' every summer on a beautiful outdoor stage, with hundreds of actors and walk-ons.

Farther south along the Trondheim Fjord lies Norway's third largest city, the technological capital of Trondheim (see page 132). In this thousand-year-old city traditional meets modern. Trondheim is one of Norway's biggest agricultural municipalities, at the same time as the city hosts one of Europe's foremost independent milieus within the maritime, technological and medical research sectors.

Nidaros, the original name of Trondheim, was an important political, religious and commercial centre from as early as the 12th century, and the many old wooden buildings by the harbour and along the river show the great degree of importance that trade has had for the city. According to tradition Scandinavia's greatest medieval building, the Nidaros Cathedral, with its magnificent sculptures and beautiful stained glass paintings, was built on the place where Saint Olav was buried after falling at the battle of Stiklestad. This made the city a destination for pilgrims for more than four centuries in the Middle Ages, and today it is a favourite destination for tourists.

RØYRVIK IS LOCATED IN THE NORTHERNMOST POINT OF NORD-TRØNDELAG, BORDERING ON SWEDEN TO THE EAST. THIS RURAL AREA CONTAINS VAST WILDER-
NESSES AND IS SURROUNDED BY STEINFJELLET IN THE WEST, BØRGEFJELL WITH ITS NATIONAL PARK IN THE NORTH, AND THE BEAUTIFUL TUNNSJØEN LAKE
IN THE SOUTH.

The Sandøla salmon river meanders lazily down through a valley in Grong, Nord-Trøndelag.

BLÅSALEN IS A BEAUTIFUL ICE GROTTO THAT APPEARS AT IRREGULAR INTERVALS UNDER A GLACIER AT THE NORTHEAST END OF BLÅHØ (1671 M ABOVE SEA-LEVEL) IN TROLLHEIMEN. THE HEAT FROM A SMALL BROOK THAT FLOWS UNDER THE GLACIER IS ENOUGH TO MELT IT FROM BELOW, AND BLÅSALEN HAS BEEN OPEN ALMOST EVERY AUTUMN SINCE 1995. SØR-TRØNDELAG.

Many of those who lived at the top of the Sleggveien road in the mining town of Røros were regarded by their contemporaries as poor people. In the small houses, which had neither cow barns nor stables, lived day labourers, widows and single parents. Sør-Trøndelag.

THE LANDSCAPE OPENS UP AT THE STOROVLINGEN MOUNTAIN LAKE IN HOLTÅLEN, SØR-TRØNDELAG.

THE LOW CLOUDS SLOWLY ENCROACH UPON THE MOUNTAINS, CREATING SHIMMERING HUES IN A BROOK IN GRÅDALEN AT RØROS. SØR-TRØNDELAG.

A CARPET OF WILD FLOWERS HAS FORMED A CANOPY OVER A CLEARING IN LIERNE, NORD-TRØNDELAG.

The Northern Lights dance across the fields on a winter's evening in Lauvsnes. Flatanger, Nord-Trøndelag.

Opposite page: A sea eagle soars over Namsfjorden in Nord-Trøndelag. With a wingspan of up to 2.5 metres the sea eagle is Norway's largest predatory bird.

TRONDHEIM

ACCORDING TO THE SAGAS Trondheim was founded by King Olav Tryggvason in the year 997, and both the city and its magnificent cathedral have a special place in the history of Norway. King Olav Haraldsson (the saint) fell in the battle of Stiklestad in 1030, and was buried by the beautiful river Nidelven, which runs through Trondheim. Tradition has it that the king was buried where the high altar of Nidaros Cathedral stands today, and in the Middle Ages the city was a destination for pilgrims as important as Santiago de Compostela in Spain. Pilgrims came here for four centuries to seek consolation, help and restitution at the canonized king's grave. Norway's monarchs have also been crowned in this national shrine – and our last two kings have been consecrated there.

Along with Nidaros Cathedral the Archbishop's Palace, the oldest secular building in the Nordic countries, has a central place in the history of Norway. Trondheim was the country's first capital city, and the Archbishop's Palace was the centre of the Norwegian ecclesiastical province. From the middle of the 12th century the Palace was a spiritual and political centre, right up until the last Catholic archbishop, Olav Engelbrektsson, had to flee the country after the

FOUNDED: 997
POPULATION: 156,000
AREA: 342 KM^2
COUNTY: SØR-TRØNDELAG

Reformation in 1537. Today parts of the Archbishop's Palace have been turned into a museum centre. In the summer season the palace is filled with many visitors, and during the annual Saint Olav Festival it is an important meeting-place – with a historical market, theatre and concerts.

From Kristiansten Fort you have a good view of the city, which is beautifully situated with the Trondheim Fjord to the north and the parkland to the south. In the centre you will find a mixture of modern buildings and picturesque wooden houses in narrow alleys. Right in the centre you will also find the beautiful Stiftsgården Palace, which is one of the Nordic countries' largest wooden buildings and has been a royal residence since 1906. Just outside the city lies the small island of Munkholmen, which has been a monastery, fortress and prison island.

Today the thousand-year-old city of Trondheim is one of Norway's most important agricultural municipalities with extensive cultivation of cereal crops, at the same time as it is one of Norway's greatest university towns, with first-class independent research milieus within the maritime, technological and medical sectors.

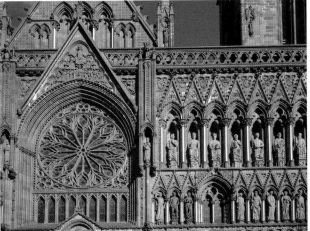

NORTHERN NORWAY

I N APRIL 1599 EIGHT HEAVILY armed naval vessels sailed from Copenhagen towards the Kola Peninsula on a mission that in retrospect could be said to be one of the most sensational and daring ones a European monarch had ever undertaken. The expedition was led by King Christian IV (albeit using an alias), and in connection with this voyage he won his first and most enduring foreign policy victory. It is no exaggeration to say that the borders Norway has in the north today were consolidated by this voyage.

On the way northward the energetic young king sailed along the same extensive coastline that is admired today by the thousands of tourists who sign up for 'the world's most beautiful voyage' with the Coastal Express from Bergen in the south to Kirkenes in the north. North Norwegian nature is varied, with dramatic island formations, deep fjords, snow-clad mountains and far-ranging plateaus that slope down to the sea, but also forest-clad valleys with lush riverbanks. Despite its location North Norway is blessed with a mild climate thanks to the Gulf Stream, and along the whole coast from the Vega Archipelago (see page 44) below the Arctic Circle and northward, birdlife abounds.

Finnmark had one of Norway's oldest settlements, the Komsa culture, which probably dates all the way back to 8000 BC. Outside Alta (see page 46) lies one of Europe's largest fields of petroglyphs, created by hunters and catchers between 6200 and 2000 years ago. Finnmark is also the core area for the indigenous Sami population, who continue to keep the traditional occupation of reindeer-tending alive. Farthest north in Finnmark lies the northernmost point on the European mainland, the popular tourist destination of the North Cape.

North Norway has many towns, and some of them are characterized by post-war buildings due to their destruction during the Second World War. With its rich array of cultural attractions and hectic nightlife, Tromsø (see page 156) is definitely worth a visit. Farther south lie the spectacular Lofoten and Vesterålen archipelagos, where the traditional fisheries have been an important subsistence basis for more than a thousand years. Today tourists can stay in the fishermen's old shanties, go on whale safaris, visit picturesque old fishing villages or find out why Henningsvær is called 'the Venice of Lofoten'.

No matter the season, it may be the continual changes in daylight that are a part of the fascination engendered by this region of Norway. On a clear summer night the midnight sun hovers like a crimson pearl above the horizon. In midwinter the red morning sky turns into dusk without ever having turned into daylight. That is when the special phenomenon known as the northern lights *(aurora borealis)* appears, flaming across the sky, constantly changing in shape and intensity, with colours ranging from luminescent green to deep red.

A pale half-moon hangs quietly over the North Cape Plateau. The picture has been taken from the northernmost point of Europe, Knivskjellodden, situated a few hundred metres farther north. Mageroya, Finnmark.

Outside Lebesby in Laksefjorden lies the Brattholmen skerry, and farther in you will find a larger island with the same name. It is no longer populated, but formerly this was both a fishing village and trading post, and here you will find a chapel and an old churchyard. On the northern side of the island lie the remains of a fortress built by German soldiers in autumn 1940. Lebesby, Finnmark

A COLONY OF CORMORANTS ON A REEF AT VÆRØY IN LOFOTEN. NORDLAND.

AURORA BOREALIS, WHICH IS THE LATIN NAME FOR THE NORTHERN LIGHTS, MEANS "THE RED MORNING LIGHT IN THE NORTH". BUT IT MIGHT AS WELL BE BLUE … LOFOTEN, NORDLAND.

Pasvik in Finnmark lies like a wedge between Russia in the east and Finland in the west, and is situated as far east as Cairo. Here the landscape is flat, with low, forested hills alternating with lakes, marshes and areas of sparse vegetation.

The Midnight Sun warms Torghatten (258 m above sea-level), known for its characteristic hole which goes right through the rock. The hole was formed during the Ice Ages, and is 160 metres long, 35 metres high and 20 metres wide. Brønnøy, Nordland.

A SEAGULL PERCHES ON A NAVIGATION MARKER IN KALDVÅGFJORDEN AT HAMARØY IN NORDLAND. IN THE BACKGROUND YOU CAN SEE THE CHARACTERISTIC PROFILE OF HAMARØYSKAFTET (613 M ABOVE SEA-LEVEL).

HEAVY CLOUD ABOVE VESTFJORDEN, BETWEEN LOFOTEN AND SALTEN IN NORDLAND.

Throughout the ages the Northern Lights have fascinated people in the northern areas and stimulated their imagination, wonderment and religious conceptions. This celestial phenomenon varies considerably in intensity, range of colours, and form, but appears most often in the last hours leading up to midnight. Behind the Northern Lights over Kvaløya in Troms you can glimpse the planet Venus.

TRÆNA IN NORDLAND IS NORWAY'S OLDEST FISHING STATION, WITH ANCIENT RELICS FROM ALMOST 9000 YEARS BACK IN TIME. THE ARCTIC CIRCLE BISECTS THE WHOLE OF THIS ARCHIPELAGO, WHICH CONSISTS OF MORE THAN 1000 ISLANDS, SKERRIES AND REEFS.

Kåfjorddalen in Troms is North Norway's biggest and most beautiful canyon. Through this valley runs the *Guolasjohka* River which comes from Lake Guolasjávri.

BETWEEN THE ISLANDS OF MOSKENES AND MOSKEN IN NORDLAND SURGES ONE OF THE WORLD'S STRONGEST MARINE CURRENTS, *MOSKENESSTRAUMEN*. THE HUGE DIFFERENCE IN HEIGHT BETWEEN LOW AND HIGH TIDE – FOUR METRES – MEANS THAT THE CURRENT CAN REACH THE AWESOME SPEED OF SIX KNOTS.

OPPOSITE PAGE: THE MIDNIGHT SUN AT 71° 10' 21" (THE NORTH CAPE). MAGERØYA, FINNMARK.

TROMSØ

EVEN THOUGH 9000-YEAR-OLD traces of settlement have been found in this area, Tromsø did not receive city status and its associated privileges before 1794, and even then the city only had a handful of inhabitants. The sagas of the Norwegian kings relate that between 1240 and 1250 King Håkon Håkonsson had a mission church built on Tromsøya. From a papal letter in 1308 we know that this church was dedicated to God's mother, Holy Mary, and that it was situated 'close to the Heathens'. It is reasonable to assume that it was not merely missionary zeal that was the motive behind its construction, but also a need to mark the fact that this was Norwegian soil. Skansen, a fortress rampart of earth and stone designed to repulse the ravages of the Karelians and Russians, probably dates from this time too.

In surface area Tromsø is Norway's most extensive urban municipality. Snow-clad mountain peaks surround the city, and with the midnight sun in summer and northern lights in the winter darkness there are few cities in the world that can offer visitors more stunning experiences of nature. From here you can go on trips to both fjord landscapes and the high seas, to wildernesses and polar mountain landscapes – or lengthier jaunts to

FOUNDED: 1794
POPULATION: 64,000
AREA: 2558 KM²
COUNTY: TROMS

the North Cape or Svalbard. The Polar Museum, which is located on an old pier from 1837, documents Tromsø's past as a centre for Arctic hunting and fishing and point of departure for expeditions to the polar regions. The city's biggest workplaces are the University of Tromsø and the University Hospital of North Norway, but the city also has a sizeable fishing fleet and varied industry with everything from shipyards to the world's northernmost brewery. The latter business benefits richly from the fact that Tromsø lives up to its nickname: the Paris of the North. The city's bars, nightclubs and restaurants have enough room for 20,000 people, which means that a third of the city's population could be out on the town simultaneously! Tromsø has a rich cultural life, with well-established cultural institutions like Hålogaland Theatre, Tromsø Symphony Orchestra and the North Norwegian Museum of Art, as well as a number of fine festivals. Among other attractions one should mention the Arctic Cathedral, which has one of Europe's largest stained glass paintings, and Tromsø Museum, with exhibits rendering a fine insight into the Sami culture.

Beyond mainland Norway

Fridtjof Nansen's ski-tracks across Greenland in 1888 and Roald Amundsen's sled-tracks to the South Pole some twenty years later symbolize both man's sense of adventure and Norway's position as a polar nation. The political desire for expansion has apparently also been limited to areas that fit our national talent – mastery of snow, ice and extreme cold. In 1925 the Svalbard Archipelago came under Norwegian jurisdiction, and in the years that followed Jan Mayen and Bouvet Island were also assigned to Norway. Norway also claims jurisdiction over Peter I's Island in the South Pacific and Queen Maud's Land in Antarctica, but both of these are covered by the Antarctic Treaty, which sets all territorial claims in this area aside. Norwegian polar imperialism suffered its most severe blow when Denmark gained jurisdiction over Greenland in 1933.

When the Dutch sailor Willem Barents discovered Bear Island in 1596, and later in the same year stepped ashore on Svalbard, he called the place Spitzbergen. He could not know that the Vikings had probably discovered Svalbard, 'the land of the cold coasts', as early as in the 12th century. This archipelago is the very embodiment of polar Norway, with permafrost up to several hundred metres beneath the ground, and 60 per cent of the land constantly covered in ice. Here we find walrus, polar bears and reindeer in a majestic landscape with high, snow-clad mountains, deep fjords and wild coastlines. Ever since the 18th century extensive hunting and catching have been pursued here. In the last few decades Norway has declared large areas of nature as protected zones on Svalbard, and most species can be found today in viable reproductive numbers, to the delight of thousands of tourists who visit these islands each year. Svalbard is also known for its large deposits of coal, and both Norwegians and Russians have been extracting this since early in the 20th century.

However, far more important than the coal deposits on Svalbard are the oil and gas deposits which since early in the 1970s have been pumped up from the bottom of the North Sea. This production has made Norway one of the world's richest countries – measured in money – but has also caused harm to life in the sea. On a flight from Great Britain to the Norwegian mainland, you will meet Norway's petroleum wealth in the form of gigantic oil platforms far out to sea.

The rich fish resources along the Norwegian coast have constituted the main subsistence activity for the coastal population for thousands of years, and as late as in the 1950s there were still 100,000 fishermen in Norway. Today there are fewer than 14,000 who have fishing as their primary occupation, and the catch of 2.5 million tonnes in 2003 puts Norway at number ten on the list of the world's biggest fishing nations. In economic terms it is the catching of cod that has the greatest value, while in the relatively new business of fish-farming it is salmon that provisionally dominates.

THE POPULATION OF A COUNTRY WHICH HAS A COASTLINE OF MORE THAN 25,000 KILOMETRES MUST NECESSARILY HAVE A CLOSE, NATURAL RELATIONSHIP WITH THE SEA, BOTH AS A BASIS FOR RESOURCES AND AS A TRANSPORTATION ARTERY.

The Norwegian oil boom began in earnest when Phillips Petroleum discovered oil in the enormous Ekofisk Field in the North Sea during the Christmas weekend of 1969. The huge, complicated concrete structures that were towed far out to sea played a central part in the further development of the Norwegian oil industry.

FEW PLACES IN EUROPE OFFER BETTER AND MORE EXCITING CONDITIONS FOR DIVING THAN HUSTADVIKA, OUTSIDE FRÆNA IN MØRE OG ROMSDAL.

The killer whale, *orcinus orca*, is common in Norwegian waters, where it often lives in social flocks of up to 20 animals. The reason killer whales form flocks in our waters is that herring is at the top of its menu, and it's most effective to collaborate in the hunt for the great schools of fish. An adult killer whale must eat many hundreds of herring each day to survive, but it can also eat seal and whale. The male can grow up to 9 metres long, weigh 6 tonnes and has a dorsal fin that can grow as high as 1.5 metres.

THE POLAR BEAR, *URSUS MARITIMUS,* CAN BE SEEN BOTH IN SVALBARD AND IN THE FROZEN SEAS AROUND THE ARCHIPELAGO. IN THE EARLY 1900S IT WAS AN ENDANGERED SPECIES, BUT THE POPULATION HAS RISEN SHARPLY AFTER IT WAS DECLARED A PROTECTED SPECIES. THE POLAR BEAR IS THE WORLD'S LARGEST PREDATORY ANIMAL LIVING ON LAND; AN ADULT MALE CAN BE MORE THAN THREE METRES LONG AND WEIGH OVER 800 KILOS. IN CONTRAST TO OTHER BEARS IT IS A PURELY PREDATORY ANIMAL AND LIVES PRIMARILY ON SEAL.

Svalbard is known for its large deposits of coal, and both Russians and Norwegians have been extracting it since the early 1900s. This is from the coal-fired power station in Longyearbyen.

THE NORWEGIAN COAST, PARTICULARLY THE STRETCH BETWEEN BERGEN AND KRISTIANSUND, AFFORDS DIVERS FROM THE WHOLE WORLD EXCEPTIONALLY VARIED AND EXCITING DIVING EXPERIENCES. HERE, ONE OF OUR MOST COLOURFUL FISH, THE CUCKOO WRASSE (*LABRUS BIMACULATUS*), HAS STUCK ITS HEAD INTO THE RIGHT-HAND CORNER OF THE PICTURE. (THIS PANORAMA IS MADE UP OF SEVERAL PICTURES FROM RUNDE AND HUSTADVIKA.)

An iceberg has frozen solid in Storfjorden on Svalbard.

On a trip with a dog team in the awe-inspiring natural surroundings at Spitzbergen. As the landscape opens up and the mountains glide past, your impressions have time to sink in. Svalbard.

Herring, *Clupea harengus*, is a silvery, plankton-eating bone fish that lives in huge schools in northern parts of the Atlantic and Pacific Oceans. The winter-spawning Norwegian herring can be over 40 cm long and 25 years old. In Norway the herring has been an important food resource for several hundred years along the whole of our extensive coast. The spawning population now stands at around 5 million tones (2002) and is one of the really store fish populations in the world. If we imagine that each herring weighs 200 grammes, we must have 25 billion herring swimming around in the Norwegian Sea and Barents Sea.

A COASTAL FISHING-BOAT SURROUNDED BY RAVENOUS SEAGULLS PLOUGHS THROUGH THE POWERFUL MOSKENESSTRAUMEN CURRENT, ON ITS WAY TO LAND. LOFOTEN, NORDLAND.

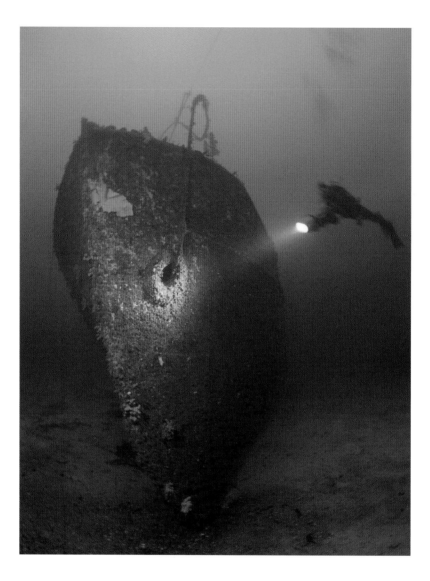

THOUSANDS OF SHIPS HAVE SUNK ALONG THE WEATHER-BEATEN NORWEGIAN COAST, BUT MOST SHIPWRECKS LIE TOO DEEP FOR TODAY'S DIVERS. THE OLD FERRYBOAT ØYGARD HAS HOWEVER BEEN SUNK BY THE SULA DIVING CLUB AND LIES AT A DEPTH OF 20 METRES OUTSIDE LANGEVÅG IN MØRE OG ROMSDAL.

2 JULY 1893 THE "DS VESTERAALEN" SET OF FROM THE QUAY IN TRONDHEIM ON A COURSE FOR HAMMERFEST, AND WITH THAT THE PIONEERING NORWEGIAN COASTAL EXPRESS WAS BORN. AS TIME PASSED, MORE SHIPS CAME INTO SERVICE, AND FOR MORE THAN A HUNDRED YEARS PEOPLE, CARS AND CARGO HAVE BEEN TRANSPORTED BETWEEN THE COASTAL TOWNS FROM BERGEN TO KIRKENES. THE COASTAL EXPRESS SHIP "MS VESTERÅLEN", HERE IN A STORM OFF THE COAST OF MØRE, IS ONE OF ELEVEN SHIPS THAT TODAY PRIMARILY CARRY ENTHUSIASTIC TOURISTS ON "THE WORLD'S MOST BEAUTIFUL VOYAGE".

The beautiful plumed anemone, *METRIDIUM SENILE*, can grow up to 20 cm high and has more than 100 tentacles.

Opposite page: In the shallows right under the famous Rundebranden, the rookery on Runde, divers can find grottos, chasms and kelp beds (*LAMINARIA HYPERBOREA*).

These maps have page references to
all the photographs in this book.
In this way you can see at any time
where in Norway the pictures
are from.

Facts about Norway

Norway is a constitutional monarchy with King Harald V as head of state. Parliamentarianism was introduced in 1884, and the Norwegian Storting (Parliament), which is divided into the Lagting and Odelsting, has 169 members. The country consists of 19 counties, which are again divided into 434 municipalities. Increased centralization of power in the State combined with extended delegation to the individual municipalities has in recent years reduced the importance of the counties. Elections to the Storting and to county assemblies and municipal councils are held alternately every two years. In the 2005–2009 electoral period seven political parties are represented in the Storting. A coalition of the Labour Party, Centre Party and Socialist Left Party formed a majority government in autumn 2005 with Jens Stoltenberg as prime minister.

The Norwegian economy is based on a combination of free market forces and governmental regulation. The government has tight control in important areas, such as the petrochemical sector, through large State-run companies. Norway is rich in natural resources such as oil, hydro-power, fish, agriculture, forestry and minerals, which has made the country very dependent upon international raw material prices, especially the price of crude oil. Norway's most important trading partners are the other Nordic countries and the EU, for although Norway has chosen to stay outside the EU along with Iceland and Liechtenstein, the country is part of the Union's inner market through the EEA agreement. As one of very few countries in the world Norway has a considerable surplus in foreign trade.

There are 4.6 million people living in Norway, divided among 1.7 million households. Most people live in and around the major cities, but there is a long and strong tradition in Norway of emphasizing the importance of a widely distributed population. This is achieved by ensuring that people are able to live in outlying areas without being cut off from opportunities in the work sector or in access to public services and cultural activities. To many people Norwegian society appears to be egalitarian and homogeneous. Among other things the welfare state that was gradually developed after the Second World War ensures free health services and compulsory 10-year education for the whole population.

Despite the fact that for long periods up to the beginning of the 19th century Norway was almost cut off from cultural impulses from the outside world, the country has developed a rich cultural tradition and given rise to great artists in many areas. Norwegian folk art has always held a strong position, and its music has inspired musicians and composers from Edvard Grieg to Jan Garbarek. The contrast between Nordic light and the Norwegian mindset can be revisited in Edvard Munch but also in a number of works by modern artists. A visible if somewhat tenuous line can be drawn from Henrik Ibsen to Jon Fosse, and Knut Hamsun's style has inspired authors throughout the world.

OFFICIAL NAME: THE KINGDOM OF NORWAY
FORM OF GOVERNMENT: CONSTITUTIONAL
MONARCHY/PARLIAMENTARY DEMOCRACY
HEAD OF STATE: HIS MAJESTY KING HARALD V
RELIGION: EVANGELIC LUTHERAN CHRISTIANITY
NATIONAL DAY: 17 MAY
CAPITAL CITY: OSLO

POPULATION: 4,604,800 (JANUARY 2006)
SURFACE AREA: 385,155 KM^2 (INCL. SVALBARD AND JAN MAYEN)
POPULATION DENSITY: 12.0 PER KM^2
LANGUAGE: NORWEGIAN (BOKMÅL AND NYNORSK).
SAMI HAS EQUAL STATUS IN SOME MUNICIPALITIES.
CURRENCY: NORWEGIAN CROWN (NOK).
GNP PER INHAB.: NOK 342,000 (2003)

Norway is the most northerly nation in Europe, and follows the North Atlantic to the west and the Scandinavian peninsula from the Skagerrak in the South via the North Sea to the Barents Sea in the north. To the east Norway borders on Sweden (1619 km), Finland (727 km) and Russia (196 km). The Norwegian mainland covers 323,758 square kilometers, sixty per cent of which are mountainous areas. Norway is known for its many fjords, and they contribute to the country's total coastline extending a staggering 25,148 kilometres!

The Gulf Stream, which comes from the Atlantic Ocean in the west, gives Norway a relatively mild climate at latitudes which would otherwise be characterized by Arctic conditions. The coastal areas have a mild, humid climate, while the inland areas east of the mountains are characterized by cold winters and hot, dry summers. This varied climate has given Norway a multiplicity of flora and fauna. Bear, wolf, reindeer, moose and musk are exotic examples of the mammals that live here. Several hundred bird species nest in Norway, but many of these migrate southward in autumn. Throughout the ages the sea, rivers and lakes have been an important source of food for humans, birds and mammals. Among the latter we also find the polar bear, the world's largest land predator. It is located on Svalbard, an archipelago in the Arctic Ocean which is under Norwegian sovereignty.

LITERATURE AND SOURCE REFERENCES:

BOOKS AND PUBLICATIONS:
Aschehougs norgeshistorie, Vol. 1–12. 1994
Norsk utenrikspolitikks historie. Universitetsforlaget 1995–1997
Bagge and Mykland: *Norge i dansketida.* Cappelen 1987
Danielsen et al.: *Grunntrekk i norsk historie.* Universitetsforlaget 1991
Furre: *Norsk historie 1914–2000.* Det Norske Samlaget 2000
Helle: *Norge blir en stat 1130–1319.* Universitetsforlaget 1974
Henriksen, Rian, Hjort, Greve: *Norges konger.* Grøndahl 1987
Kristiansen: *Dette er Norge.* Statistics Norway 2003
Libæk and Stenersen: *Norges historie fra istid til i dag.* Dinamo 2003

NET-BASED SOURCES:
Alta Museum (www.alta.museum.no)
Bergen Municipality (www.bergen.kommune.no)
Caplex (www.caplex.no)
Fortidsminneforeningen (www.stavechurch.com)
Kristiansand Municipality (www.kristiansand.kommune.no)
Oslo Municipality (www.oslo.kommune.no)
Central Office of Historic Monuments (www.riksantikvaren.no)
Stavanger Municipality (www.stavanger.kommune.no)
Stiftelsen Bryggen (www.stiftelsenbryggen.no)
Tromsø Municipality (www.tromso.kommune.no)
Trondheim Municipality (www.trondheim.kommune.no)
UNESCO (www.unesco.no)
Vega as world heritage (www.verdensarvvega.no)
The world heritage of Røros (www.verdensarvenroros.no)

LIST OF PICTURES:

Per Eide (www.pereide.no) is responsible for the selection of photographs in this book. He has taken most of the pictures himself, while he has chosen the rest with the utmost care from historical archives and from his most proficient colleagues.

Bergen Municipality: page 76
The Museum of National History at Frederiksborg: page 19
The Kon-Tiki Museum: page 30
Kristiansand Municipality: page 92
The Museum of Cultural History (Univ. of Oslo): page 11, 15
Minnesota Historical Society: page 23
O. Væring Eftf. AS: page 16, 21, 24 (Edvard Munch/Munch-museet/BONO 2006)
Oslo Municipality: page 114
Samfoto: page 4, 8 (Asgeir Helgestad), 93al, 93dr, 98, 99, 115ar, 155 (Bård Løken), 12 (Øystein Søbye), 33 (Morten Løberg), 31, 45 (Tore Wuttudal), 103, 112 (Asle Hjellbrekke), 149 (Bjørn Jørgensen), 44, 93dl, 130 (Pål Hermansen), 141 (Rolf Sørensen), 161 (Paul Sigve Amundsen), 115al, 115dl, 115ar (Espen Bratlie), 93ar (Bjørn-Owe Holmberg)
Scanpix: page 25 (Scanpix), 27 (Sygma), 29 (ukjent), 34 (Pierre Villard/Sipa)
The National Administration Service: page 178,179
Stavanger Municipality: page 74
Tromsø Municipality: page 156
Trondheim Municipality: page 132

© Font Forlag 2006

Graphic design and cover: Mona Dahl
Maps: Geir Tandberg Steigan
Photo editor: Per Eide
Production consultant: Rune Samuelsen
Repro: Iris Assistanse as
Paper: Gallerie Art Silk (150 gram)
Printing and binding: Graphicom

First edition

Second printing

ISBN 978-82-8169-005-9

ISBN 978-82-8169-004-2 (Norwegian edition)
ISBN 978-82-8169-011-0 (German edition)
ISBN 978-82-8169-012-7 (Spanish edition)

www.fontforlag.com

The word 'font' comes from the Latin *fons*, which means source or fountain. Today the word is mostly used in the sense of typeface, the typographical appearance of a set of letters or symbols. As early as in ancient Egypt there existed two typefaces (*hieratic* and *demotic*). These were hieroglyphs that were either etched in stone or written on papyrus.

When Johann Gutenberg invented the art of book-printing in the 1430s, it was necessary to standardize the written symbols. The writing style of that time, *Gothic,* was extremely complex and ornate, and in due course simplified versions emerged. Around 1890 the Gothic style of writing disappeared from daily use, and *Antiqua* became the dominant group of typefaces. Antiqua is based on the Roman monumental writing style; each letter consists of a basic line, a hairline and small enhancements called *serifs*. The other main group of typefaces today is called *Grotesque.* This was first used in 1916 by the English printer William Caslon III, and is characterized by the letters having equally thick lines and lacking serifs. Most typefaces in general use belong either to the Antiqua group or to the Grotesque group. These two groups can be further divided into sub-groups according to how much space each letter takes up regardless of appearance (for example an M and an I), or to whether the space needed by the individual letter is related to its appearance. The latter style, called *proportional fonts*, was developed by the American newspaper industry to save printer's ink and paper, which explains the name of one of the most used typefaces in this category, *Times.* Today proportional fonts dominate production of newspapers, magazines and books.

Font Forlag uses the *Trajan* Antiqua typeface in its logo. This was developed by the American Carol Twombly in 1989, and was stylistically inspired by the 40-metre high Trajan Column, which was erected in Rome between 106 and 113 AD to commemorate the Emperor Trajan's military conquests. Ascending this column, which has a diameter of almost four metres, runs a 200-metre long spiral band of magnificent reliefs. The base of the column is decorated with the finest examples of Roman script and sculpture. These inscriptions are regarded by many as the most important inspiration for the various Antiqua scripts.

This book has been set in a *Bembo* type, an Antiqua typeface named after the Italian cardinal and author Pietro Bembo (1470–1547). When one of the most renowned printers of the Italian Renaissance, Aldus Manutius, was going to print his work *de Aetna* in 1496, he adopted a new typeface developed by Francesco Griffo. He was one of the first to gradually leave the more complex calligraphic style, and he developed the simpler, more stylized typeface we know and use today. In 1929 Stanley Morison was inspired by Francesco Griffo's mode of expression when he developed the Bembo typeface, a beautiful, timeless font that is often used in books.

FONT FORLAG